THE
FIVE
MINUTE
GARDEN

THE
FIVE
MINUTE
GARDEN

How to garden
in next to no time

Laetitia Maklouf

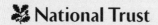 National Trust

For my Rotter, with love.

First published in the United Kingdom in 2020 by
National Trust Books
43 Great Ormond Street
London WC1N 3HZ
An imprint of Pavilion Books Company Ltd

ISBN: 9781911358916

A CIP catalogue record for this book is available from the
British Library.

25 24 23 22 21 20
10 9 8 7 6 5 4 3

Reproduction by Rival Colour Ltd, UK
Printed and bound by GPS Group P.E., Slovenia

This book can be ordered direct from the publisher at the
website: www.pavilionbooks.com, or try your local bookshop.

Contents

Introduction

Let me tell you a story. It's about a garden. The garden was large for its city location, and its owner had made sure that every inch of it was full to bursting with flowers. There was neither rhyme nor reason to the placement of each plant. Nature weaved its merry tapestry in the borders and the place buzzed with life. It was beautiful and magical and overgrown; a law unto itself, and people loved it, soaking up its summer bounty. But its owner spent her time swinging wildly between love and loathing for her garden. She loved the wildness and the colour, but it also made her feel panicked and overwhelmed. The grass grew out of control and her children opted for the park instead of the garden; there was nowhere to sit and relax, or eat, or walk about. The garden had got away from her and the balance between human and nature, represented by a garden, had got wildly out of whack.

This was me a few years ago, looking forlornly out of the window, with three small children to look after and wondering if I would ever have time to stay on top of the garden, along with everything else that needed my attention. It seemed impossible; I was accustomed to gardening at weekends or setting aside entire days to 'deal with the garden', spending hours at a time getting things back under control, only to find myself in the same situation a couple of weeks later. I stopped gardening altogether for a while, and then I made the commitment to redesign the garden with the intention of minimising my workload. The flowerbeds were dramatically reduced, and I kept to a painfully tiny palette of plants to fill them. I got rid of any and all containers smaller than 40cm (16in) wide and put in a path around the edge of the garden so that I'd have easy access to the flowerbeds from both sides. And guess what? The same thing happened. That first summer, as I was enjoying the new space, that old feeling of being overwhelmed returned, just as strongly as it had before, except that this time, because my garden was no longer 'wild' there was nowhere to hide, and when I ran out of time to tend to it, it actually looked worse than before; bare and unkempt s opposed to abundant and messy.

I realised changing my garden wasn't enough; I needed to change the way I interacted with it too. So, I decided that instead of trying to carve out large tracts of time in my busy life once in a while, instead I would go out and do something small every day. I looked carefully at my schedule and realised that in all honesty, I had no more than five minutes every day to give to the garden. I started to go out every day, rain or shine, whether I felt like it or not, and do something for my garden for five minutes. I would pick random things – the quickest, easiest things first, and then I began to tackle larger endeavours, five minutes at a time, over a period of days. Sometimes I would spend more than five minutes, caught up in the moment, and find I had actually done an hour. Often I would do less than five minutes; three minutes of weeding squeezed in right at the end of a day, or two minutes of deadheading snatched while the children weren't pawing at me. After a couple of months of this, I looked outside and realised this approach was working far better than I could ever have imagined. The garden was cared-for and inviting, and the lawn was mown, and my children were playing on it. But more importantly, I was enjoying my own space too – actually sitting down in my own garden. Finally, it was doing the job for which it was intended; to be a happy space for me and my family to enjoy.

The purpose of this book is to take the decision-making out of the process and act as a springboard to catapult you out into your outside space; it's packed with five-minute things you might want to try over the gardening year, which you can pick and choose at random when you have five minutes to spare. These little bursts of activity are set under different headings: Spruce, Chop, Nurture, Fuss and Project. I tend do one thing from each heading over the course of the week. You can find the formula I follow at the back of this book (see pages 168–171), but everyone is different, and the important thing is just to begin – just pick one thing at random from the relevant month in this book, and go out and start on that, because at some point in the very near future, you'll look behind you and realise how very far you have come.

Happy gardening.

A note about the five-minute thing

If you decide to use the five-minute approach to gardening, you should know that the timing aspect can be pretty elastic. There are days when you'll have the time (and inclination) to stay and keep going for much longer than five minutes, and there will be other days, when you can literally only manage 300 seconds. The point is that we can ALL stop what we're doing and go outside for five minutes. That's the idea that gets us out there and doing something positive. Yes, you can take this whole thing totally literally if you like – set a timer and do proper five-minute bursts – and your garden will look lovely, and you will benefit too, because you made the time to go outside. But you can also let the mood take you for longer, and you'll be able to go a bit deeper, and understand your garden a bit better ... it's not set in stone; it's up to you.

Important things
In order to use your five minutes effectively, you need to work towards:

Having tools, outdoor shoes and gloves easily accessible.
Having water easily accessible, in cans or a hose, ready to use (see page 83).
Having only large containers (wider than 40cm/16in in diameter).

January

*'The shortest day has passed, and whatever
nastiness of weather we may look forward to in
January and February, at least we notice
that the days are getting longer.'*
Vita Sackville-West

Let's begin by saying that too much messing about with the
garden at this time of year can actually do more harm than
good; trampling all over your borders, for example, will cause
compaction, while a flurry of seed-sowing will, in the long run,
just leave you deeply anxious and depressed. So, with that in
mind, here are some gentle five-minute endeavours for those
itching for action and needing to get out and sniff the air.

SPRUCE

Start at the back door
If you really can't bear the idea of stepping outside (and I
wouldn't blame you in a wet, cold miserable January), just use
this trick to get you going. Start at the back door. Put your
gloves, coat and boots on, look outside and go directly to the
first thing your eyes fall upon that's looking a bit like it needs
some attention: it could be a gone-over perennial you haven't
dealt with; or it could be something you've left in the garden

that shouldn't be there. Whatever it is, go directly towards it and deal with it. Once that's done, you'll probably want to do some more ... but if not, then just go inside. It's all good.

Sweep away

Yes, you're still sweeping – not leaves, but possibly snow and definitely the general detritus that seems to build up at this time of year, firstly because it is generally wet or damp, and things *stick* when it's wet or damp, and secondly because when there is less to look at in the garden, one's eye gets caught by the rather more mundane stuff. So, sweep away Cinderella, and regard this as your five minutes of wholesomeness before you retreat back indoors to eat the rest of the Stilton.

Weed every day you can

Honestly, honestly, if you can do a bit of judicious sprucing up in the borders or pots every day, then unwanted weeds will never become a problem for you ... they just won't. Unless it's snowing or pitifully cold, then a bit of weeding, with a podcast and a kneeler will do all the good things for your mind, body and soul. Put a timer on, and some headphones, and just go for it.

Gritting

It really is a good idea to get your grit on at this time of year, firstly because it is bound to become icy or snowy when you least expect it, and secondly because it is an awful bore to spend the new year with a broken leg. Go out and get some bags of grit and put them, together with a pair of gloves and a shovel or trowel, wherever you think they'll be most needed when the time comes.

Pond care

Check your pond (or body of water). If you have fish then it's a good idea to float a football on the surface to stop it icing over. And if you haven't done so already, take five minutes to clear a few leaves out. This five-minute leaf removal system is a good thing to keep going with (like brushing your teeth every morning) whenever you pass your pond or happen to be lurking near it. A pool clear of soggy, mouldering leaves will lift even the most neglected of gardens due to light refraction; it's one of those endeavours that pays great dividends.

CHOP

Brown crispy or soggy bits

You may have ignored all this at the end of last year. You may have been given this book for Christmas and decided to 'do something about the garden' for the first time. Whatever the case, if there are brown, crispy or soggy bits of plant in your garden that don't look fabulous, then go out and take five minutes to chop them down right now. Immediately. Chopping away old stuff is one of the best ways to get to know your garden intimately.

Bring in some winter scent

Here are my favourite scented winter plants that you can and should chop bits off to make you feel better when it's all glum and dark. If you don't own any of these then I suggest rectifying that error. The *Sarcococca* is probably the easiest of them all – happy in a pot and seemingly oblivious to poor treatment and conditions – but they are all winners.

- *Sarcococca confusa* (sweet box)
- *Daphne odora* 'Aureomarginata' (winter daphne)
- *Lonicera* × *purpusii* 'Winter Beauty' (winter-flowering honeysuckle)

One sprig from any of these beauties, put into a vase and brought into the warm, will envelop your home in the most glorious scented cuddle. Do it. Now.

NURTURE

....

Supermarket basil pots

You need a dose of summer. You need it. Do this, and
your pot of supermarket basil will last for ages, rather
than becoming a throw-away item within days.

Take one large supermarket basil plant, remove it from its
pot and divide it gently and carefully into three sections.
Plant each section with a little more multi-purpose
compost in a separate pot, similar in size to the basil's
original home. Firm gently and water in well. Let everything
bed down for a week or so, and then start harvesting your
three pots of basil, removing single, large, luscious leaves
and tips to encourage bushy growth and allow light to the
emerging baby leaves below. Enjoy this taste of summer,
indoors for weeks on end, and repeat *ad infinitum*.

FUSS

....

Check your houseplants

Knowing where your houseplants come from is the easiest
way to establish their care needs. Desert plants (such as cacti,
succulents and so on) can deal with a lot temperature-wise but
you'll kill them if you over-water them. If in doubt (and

particularly in winter) less is more. A cactus or succulent will often come back from a shrivelled corpse if you have forgotten to water, but will seldom survive an overzealous hand with the watering can. Tropical or rainforest plants, like most orchids, *Monstera* (Swiss cheese plant) and figs need a warmer environment with moist air, as you might expect. This means spraying the leaves when you remember and keeping things pretty dry in the pot too, especially during the winter.

Obsess about your winter gaps

This is a very good way to fuss as it simply involves staring out of the window, or at a few hastily taken photos of your flowerbeds. Think about how you might improve your outlook for winter and then consider putting in some of these winter wonders, which, by the way, will look good all summer too:

Hellebores: evergreen leaves, out-of-this-world gorgeous flowers in winter.

Ferns: evergreen of course. Never not chic.

Scented winter shrubs (see page 14).

Topiary and hedging: whether evergreen or deciduous, these provide a solid framework in the garden when there's nothing else to look at.

Order seeds for the spring

Don't go mad now; it's very easy to bite off more than you can chew. Just bear in mind that the average packet of seeds could fill a small garden, so you need to be conservative and strict with yourself. Create a longlist, and then try to chop it in half. Then chop it in half again. Here are my favourite seeds to sow in the spring.

Cobaea scandens **(cup and saucer vine)**: can be sown as early as January indoors and will cover a large wall, with zero help from you, within weeks. Available in white or purple.

Centaurea **(cornflower)**: the most obliging of subjects. I like to sow them direct in April, but you can also start them off earlier, indoors. If you love them, then you might want to sow some more in late summer too, for bigger, earlier flowers next year.

Euphorbia oblongata **(Balkan spurge)**: the most wonderful filler plant, both in the border and the vase. I sow a tray or two in February or March and plant out into each and every gap.

Nasturtium: so easy; just poke the seeds into the ground in March and you're away. After this initial effort, they will self-seed beautifully around the garden, and you will find yourself pulling the odd one out, rather than putting them in.

Nicotiana **(tobacco plant)**: it is well worth the effort of sowing these tiny seeds for pots on the terrace as the scent is out of this world. I sow them indoors in March or April.

Do remember though, that you don't have to raise seedlings yourself; most things can be bought as tiny plug plants, which you then pot on and plant out, these include:

Alpine strawberries (see pages 48–49)
Chilli peppers (see page 30)
Tomatoes (see page 31)

Snowdrops
Order snowdrops if you don't have any. You need them. You do.

Twigs for support
Hazel is being harvested at the moment and it's a really good idea to stock up on some twigs and/or bean poles for the year ahead. Hazel twigs can be bent into half-moon shapes and pushed into the ground to prevent plants falling over onto lawn edges. They can also be fashioned into domes through which plants can grow. Most of all though, a few twigs, plunged into the ground, or around the side of a large container and tied together at the top, make the prettiest obelisk for sweet peas or other climbing plants. Try to get hold of some now.

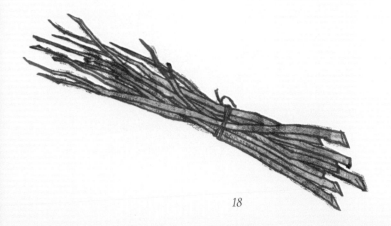

Project: Microgreens

This is the easiest way to get gardening without getting wet, cold or putting your back out. It also gives a lovely punch to every dish you make. You will need:

· a seed tray set within another larger tray for watering
· some multi-purpose compost
· some seeds; I adore radish, rocket, basil, coriander and mizuna, or you can buy a mixture of seeds specially packaged as microgreens.

Fill your tray with compost, removing any big bits and tapping it firmly to remove any pockets of air. Fill up the bottom tray with water for a few hours until the surface of the compost is damp.

Now sprinkle your seeds liberally over the top, aiming for an even coverage. You don't need to worry about spacing here because you'll be harvesting the greenery before it has a chance to need any space.

Cover the seeds thinly with a bit more compost, sieving it over the top.

Given the warmth of your kitchen, the seeds will germinate fast, and in a couple of weeks you'll be snipping and sprinkling just like all the posh chefs. You can also do this on kitchen paper, without any compost, but you must make sure the paper never dries out.

Deep clean the shed

This is serious January stuff and I include it here in my five-minute book because I do it over a series of days, in five-minute bursts. It involves buckets of steaming hot water which is nice in the cold, and a certain steely resolve. Work from top to bottom and left to right. Start at the door and clear everything to your immediate left. Use boiling hot soapy water with some peppermint essential oil, and scrub every surface, including window and door frames. Dry with a clean towel, wipe everything that lives in that particular space and replace it. Your shed will be sparkling clean over a short period, but much more importantly, you will feel like a GOD.

Mulching

Are you mulching? If not, then see pages 154–155 and begin, remembering that the only bad time to mulch is when it's baking hot or freezing cold. It's the very loveliest thing you can do for your garden. One trug or barrowful a day, or even every week as part of your Friday project, will have the endeavour completed before you know it.

Turning your compost

The rather boring truth about compost, as with so many things, is that hard work pays off. There are plenty of people who feel that turning a compost heap is a waste of time; they simply skim off any unbroken-down matter and take the good stuff from the middle. That's fine, but if you want lots of evenly decomposed black stuff, relatively quickly, then turning your heap is essential to keep oxygen levels up, thereby speeding up decomposition. This is hard work, but it doesn't have to take ages; so enlist some help, put on your filthiest T-shirt (you'll get hot) and dash out with a fork. Quickly remove the top layer of your compost from the heap and then attack the rest, forking out the material that lies around the edges of the bin or pen. Now disperse all the remaining compost, putting a few forkfuls into a wheelbarrow for plonking on top, and pushing the rest out to the sides. Toss the stuff you removed at the beginning back into the centre, and finally put your wheelbarrow load on top. This is not a fine art, just a bit of manic pitch-forkery, so don't spend more than 40 minutes at it. You are aiming to get the outside to the middle and vice versa, safe in the knowledge that a little effort is infinitely better than doing nothing at all, and that you are definitely burning off your Sunday lunch.

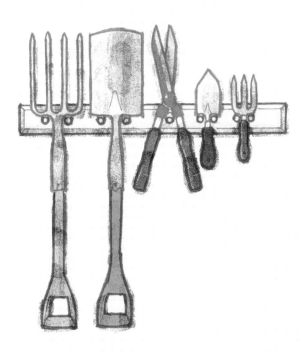

February

'In seed time learn, in harvest teach,
in winter enjoy.'
William Blake

Do you feel guilty when you simply wait winter out? I used to,
until I suddenly realised the bliss of stopping, reflecting, and
frankly doing very little. Here, though, are some of the things
I *do* manage in the freezing times; more to get me outside and
ruddy-cheeked than any urgent horticultural reason.

SPRUCE

Weeding

Not to panic you or anything, but things are waking up in
the garden, big time, and if you want to stay on top of stuff,
it's best to get a handle on the situation right now. I use my
square-metre method for weeding, in which I take one small
area at a time and just concentrate on that one space. This
works for me as it reduces overwhelm and, if you mulch
immediately afterwards, is one of the most satisfying things you
can do for yourself in five minutes. Obviously weeding is a little
more complicated, and mulching is well-nigh impossible when
you have bulbs emerging, but still, be steadfast in your removal
of any unwanted plants, and you will thank yourself later.

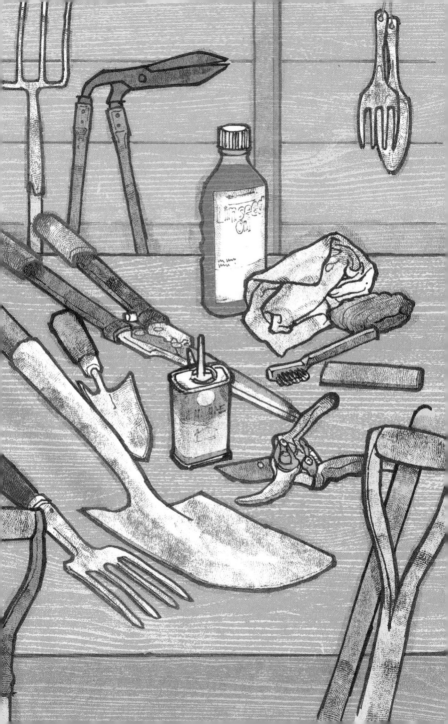

Safety first

If the weather is dastardly then you're going to need to keep yourself and others from slipping by being boringly sensible and gritting any hard surfaces. See pages 12–13 for info on being ready for this eventuality.

The cleaning of tools

I'm well aware that this is the kind of tip that people read but never actually use. Just know that if you look after your tools and they work properly, your enjoyment and ease in the garden will be exponentially magnified. Eliminate dirt from your tools with water and a cloth, and then use wire wool or a sanding block on all your blades – secateurs, choppers, loppers and so on, if needed. This is to remove grime and rust. Give them a light coating of linseed oil and then sharpen with a sharpening stone or sharpening 'pen' tool, which is so tiny that you don't have to take your secs or shears apart. The best storage for tools is hanging on a wall so you can access them really quickly, but if that's not possible, use a bucket or three, filled with sand and plunge your (clean) tools into it after each use. The sand will keep them dry.

The clearing of gutters

Any gutter you can reach is worth clearing while you have the time. You'll be amazed at how full they are with compost ... how on earth does compost get up there? Well, it's decomposing leaf-matter, and you can simply use it on your flowerbeds.

The sluicing of bins

While you're in spring-cleaning mode, nothing will make you feel quite so virtuous as cleaning out your bins. I use a bucket of boiling-hot water laced with a few drops of Sal Suds and about 20 drops of tea tree oil or similar. Pour the whole lot in, swish it around and pour directly down the drain. Dry upside down. Rubber gloves essential, smug looks optional.

CHOP

Prune your clematis

I used to be royally put off growing clematis because of all the mind-boggling pruning instructions. Here is the information I have distilled from hours of reading on the interweb, and it works for me:

Is your clematis one of the large, evergreen ones that flowers early in spring? If so, then leave it alone.

Is it starting to flower in late spring and early summer? If so, then perform some surgery in late winter or very early spring, removing all the dead stuff and cutting any living shoots back to just above a good strong bud – the bud you like the best.

Does it flower in the summer and early autumn? If so, then this is the easiest one to prune, just hack the whole thing back to just above the bud that's nearest to 20cm (8in) above the ground, also in late winter or early spring.

Prune your fruit trees if you haven't already

Most fruit trees need pruning in the cold months, when there are fewer pesky critters, spores and such-like to take advantage of freshly cut wood. My primary advice here is to contact a professional to come and deal with the situation. It is skilled (and not un-dangerous) work. But if you want to have a go then the golden rule is that you are trying to create a framework whereby air can circulate, with fewer, larger branches rather than millions of little ones. To this end it is vital that you do not just give the tree a 'haircut'; this will encourage it to produce loads of tiny shoots, congesting the tree. Different methods for different trees are beyond the realms of this book, so read up on the rules for your particular tree carefully and proceed with caution.

Perennials

There are going to be some perennials still standing of course ... the ones you couldn't quite bear to cut down. For me it's always the *Verbena bonariensis*, which I leave to look after itself until I suddenly spy new sideshoots appearing halfway up the main stem and know that I have to take the situation in hand. I want the new growth to come from the ground, not halfway up last year's plant. Chop, chop, chop.

NURTURE

Sow some parsley

Parsley can be sown and grown entirely indoors if you've no outdoor space. I remember baulking at constant instructions to sow '6-12 weeks before the last frost'. (Do I look like a mystic?)

So I ignore all that and sow, sans propagator, in February, in my kitchen.

Parsley takes a while to germinate, so always sow more than you think you want, and do use plugs or peat-free Jiffy-7 pellets, so you can remove the seedling into a larger pot, together with the soil in which it was born, and it will never know the difference.

Sow on the surface of some very fine, gritty seed compost (make sure you water it before you sow). Put two seeds in each cell, in opposite corners if possible. Cover with perlite.

Be patient; the seeds can take up to six weeks to emerge, and some won't appear at all, which I swear is normal. You need to keep things constantly moist, and if your plug tray comes with a clear plastic lid, then so much the better, but as soon as you see action, remove any lids and keep watch over your babies until they look ready to move to larger pots (push one out of its plug and check for a good root system before you do this).

You can then either keep them in containers or plant them in some good, rich, weed-free soil, once the weather is being civil. Variety-wise, flat-leaf parsley tastes better but curly parsley looks gloriously hummocky on any window-sill.

Nurture your relationships

Doesn't matter if you 'do' Valentine's day or not, it's still important to let people know that they are thought about. A long-tom pot (see page 172) planted with heavily scented lily bulbs would have this gardener weak at the knees. Plant bulbs at twice their depth, giving each one a little bed of sharp sand to prevent rotting. Cover them up with more compost and mulch the top of the whole thing with small gravel. Label or tag it thoughtfully and plonk it on your loved-one's front step before you give it a good watering. You could then add a small box with a large emerald inside it if you feel like it.

Plant evergreen containers

You're going to love me forever for this tip. You see, if you manage to steer yourself away from the bedding sections of the garden centre and plant something permanent and evergreen in your empty containers (and I hope they are large ones), then you'll be giving yourself the ultimate five-minute gift: a beautiful container that you never have to change or do anything to, but which will give you pleasure and loveliness for years to come. Here are my top three evergreens for containers:

Hellebores: sultry, unusual with lots of speckled, moody colours. The leaves give interest throughout the year, and you can push bulbs in the gaps too.

Ferns: large pots with ferns in them are exquisitely sophisticated. They look amazing flanking an entrance or path, or singly, as a focal point. The best ferns for the job are large- or medium-sized evergreen ferns, such as *Woodwardia fimbriata*, *Polystichum setiferum* and *Dryopteris affinis*. Keep the pot elevated or use a shallow plastic pan within a larger pot (ferns don't need a deep root run).

Muehlenbeckia: despite being difficult to spell, my love for this plant is unwavering. It will tumble over the sides of a pretty pot or urn as if it has been there for a century and it will also climb if you help it by tying it in.

A plant isn't truly in your garden if it's not in its space

When you buy a new plant (which is inevitable at this time of year), know exactly where it's destined for, and deal with it immediately. I find that if I leave new plants for any length of time they simply lose their allure somehow and I'm less inclined to look after them. Once you've got a plant home, re-pot it, or plant it at once.

Bedded bliss

The ultimate in armchair gardening for me is ordering the bedding for my terrace containers. If you've never bought plug-plants before then welcome to heaven, in which all the hard work of raising from seed has been done for you by experts, and yet you receive plants in bulk, for much less than you'd pay for them if you got them, later and larger, from a nursery. My favourites are:

Argyranthemum: an absolute stunner of a daisy which
  just goes on and on and on, with a bit of deadheading.
Nemesia and Diascia: both fabulously easy and end up
  making delightful frothy mounds in your pots. Good
  scent too.
Lobelia: such joy from the tiny sprays of floral goodness.
Euphorbia 'Diamond Frost': the hardest-working,
  loveliest-looking plant ever. Always covers up ugly
  plant 'legs' (see page 46) and the froth-factor is through
  the roof.

With all of these (and all the other things I haven't had room to
mention) feeding and watering is the key to profusion, more of
which on page 83.

Plant snowdrops

It's time to plant snowdrops, which, if you ordered them, will
have been lifted out of the ground after flowering and sent to
you. Dig a nice deep hole for each one and put some grit in it.
You want the soil level to come 1cm (⅜in) or so above where the
stalk starts to become green. If you're planting in a container
then John Innes No.2 potting compost with some added grit
will be appreciated. In a lawn, remove a plug of turf with a
bulb planter, loosen the soil as before, add grit and back-fill
with John Innes No.2, or the soil from the removed plug,
sans the grass.

Chillies

These wonderful little bushes are fabulously easy from seed and
can be brought indoors to over-winter and resurrected for the
following year. Use the same method for sowing as for tomatoes
(opposite) and go for a dwarf variety, such as 'Pikito'.

Tomatoes

I include tomatoes in *The 5-Minute Garden*, because although you may only grow a few, they will most certainly be the best tomatoes you have ever tasted, and if you are an old hand at growing them, then they will be easy to factor into your daily endeavours. There are, though, tomatoes and tomatoes, and for the purposes of the five-minute garden, our attitude to edibles has to remain firmly rooted in seeking the tastiest morsels rather than feeding the screaming hoards. With that in mind, it's sensible to choose a tumbling variety that you can grow in a container or hanging basket, and that doesn't need too much faffing over (apart, of course, from the inevitable watering and feeding commitments).

Find a tumbling variety, such as 'Cherry Falls', and sow no more than a three or four seeds into individual pots or peat-free Jiffy-7 pellets, covering lightly with compost. Germinate the seeds in the warmth and light of your kitchen, using a propagator with a lid, or fashion a humid atmosphere over each pot using clear plastic sandwich bags and elastic bands. As soon as the seeds appear, remove the lid or bags, along with any bottom heat you have going on, and grow the seedlings on slowly until they have a few leaves and are ready to harden off (see page 42).

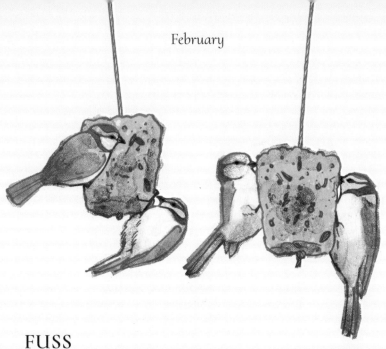

FUSS

Undo your wreath

'Fess up – you haven't done it have you? It's in a dark corner,
going crispy and dying, or no, perhaps it's still on the door?
That's okay; we can totally be friends because SAME. But look,
now is the time to tackle it. I'm not going to tell you how to
dispose of a wreath, but I am going to beg you to fuss around a
bit with the wire – rather than just cutting it up, try to unravel
it so that you can reuse it next year, or for some other project.
I sound like my granny who had a drawer full of old elastic
bands, and made 'notebooks' out of scrap paper held together
with bulldog clips – and I'm glad, because that's where we all
need to be heading if we want to live in a world that isn't
drowning in rubbish. So, spend a few moments unravelling,
cutting up and composting, and then stash the whole lot
away for next time around.

Project: Fat balls for the birds

I've made these several different ways, but I'm going to share the quickest and easiest way here, in the spirit of five-minute gardening. You need:

· bird seed (available at garden centres)
· lard or beef suet (available at larger supermarkets)
· string
· old yoghurt pots or other small containers

Have the lard at room temperature and squidge it with your hands until it forms a thick paste.

Add the birdseed and mix it in, so that everything comes together into tennis-ball-sized spheres.

If you're reusing plastic containers like yoghurt pots, put a hole in the bottom of each and thread some string through the hole, knotting it at the base of the pot.

Fill the pots up with the mixture, so that the string stays in a straight line and comes up and out through the mixture at the top of each pot; put them in the fridge to harden.

Once they have set, you just need to snip the yoghurt pot away with scissors and hang the fat ball off a nearby tree. Hanging fat balls like this is infinitely preferable to leaving a ball on a bird table, as it means the big brutish birds (and the squirrels) can't get to it so easily.

Cut some string into lengths

Did you ever think you'd be the sort of person to carry bits of string in your pockets? Me neither, but I swear this is such a brilliant time-saver. Spend five minutes cutting a ball of garden twine into lengths of about 30–40cm (12–16in), and then stash them in your coat pockets, ready for action as and when you need to tie things in or up.

Tree planting

A few Februarys ago, I decided on nothing more than a whim to plant three trees in my lawn. It was one of the best gardening decisions I have ever made, transforming my garden from a tame, rather boring space into something with interest and personality. February when everything is still rather bare outside is a great time to think about this kind of thing, and determine whether you have enough vertical accents in your space. Take a photo on your phone and then select 'edit' where you should find a 'mark-up' function. You can scribble in anything you want and get an idea of what it would look like.

Here are some suggestions for lawn trees, if you decide it's just the thing for you:

Amelanchier: the prettiest-ever, butterfly-like blooms in April and gorgeous autumn colour.

Crab apple: many, many varieties to choose from – all have those dinky little fruits that look lovely on the tree and with which you can also make delicious jelly.

Prunus: particularly the very loveliest *P. × subhirtella* 'Autumnalis', a small ornamental cherry that blossoms through the winter months.

Japanese acer: delicate foliage with stunning autumnal hues and slow growth habits make this a real feature. Some varieties will even grow happily in pots.

Dealing with unwanted guests

The fact that your garden or outside space 'belongs' to you is merely a human construct. Foxes, squirrels and neighbouring cats just see it as part of their territory, so ditch the umbrage and put some water-squirters into your area. These react to movement, shooting out a quick jet of water to deter lurkers.

March

'When it is summer in the light
and winter in the shade'.
Charles Dickens

March is where we expect to see spring appear, and yet it is
May which often gives us that pleasure. With that in mind, I'm
putting a large range of suggestions here, including perhaps the
most important one of all which is:

Go easy!
If the weather is being beastly then go with your gut and shut
the door. Gardening in the snow is actually counter-productive,
both for your garden and for your soul.

SPRUCE

Houseplant watering
Light levels will be rising, even if temperatures are not, and
in your indoor environment where you control the heating
that means your houseplants will be waking up a little. Start
watering your succulents, cacti and other houseplants a little
more regularly than hitherto, and if you see active growth, then
a half-measure of your chosen feed can now be administered.

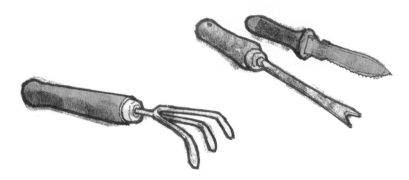

Container watering

If the weather is being nice to you, then gently pick up a watering can and tend to your containers. Don't feed, because you still have April to get through, and 'Sometimes it snows in April', as the song goes. You don't want a whole load of soft, sappy growth being zapped by damnable frost and snow, do you?

Weeding in earnest

There is always weeding to be done. *Always*. But if you have clement weather then you really can steal a march on the job *in* March. Weeds are emerging, but not rampant, and if you do just five minutes of hoeing a day you'll weaken them enough to ensure they're not a problem going forward.

A word about your soil

Try your best not to tread on your soil too much. If you tread on it, the soil becomes compacted and its delicate structure, full of tiny little holes burrowed by worms and other micro-organisms, will be ruined. Try to make it your thing to carry around a plank of wood with you – doesn't need to be long, but if you need to step onto your soil the wood will disperse your weight somewhat. The other trick when you have big flowerbeds is to place a permanent stepping-stone or two at regular intervals, so that you can use these to plant yourself while you do your weeding, planting, and so on.

CHOP

Take your pick

Are there beauteous bulbs peeking out of the ground? There should be – crocuses perhaps, miniature daffodils and irises – all of these are there for your delectation if only you would pick them and take them indoors. Picking flowers is essential, particularly if it is cold. A crocus will open up in the warmth of your house and pump out its honey scent at nose level; you'll never experience that outside unless you get on your hands and knees in the mud. So, pick away, and note down any bulbs you want more of so that you can plant them in the autumn.

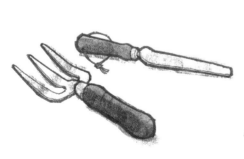

Pruning hydrangeas

This is a nice easy outing for your secateurs. Most hydrangeas will be perfectly happy without any pruning at all, but if you think that your plant is under-performing, or out of shape, then pruning it could be just the ticket to billowing clouds of blossoms this summer.

Mop-heads and lace-caps (*H. macrophylla*) have thick, toothed, heart-shaped leaves. Blooms are usually blue, pink or purple. Lace-caps have tiny fertile flowers surrounded by larger infertile ones, and mop-heads, as the name suggests, have large blooms all over. These should be pruned in late summer by removing weaker stems.

Oak-leaved hydrangeas (*H. quercifolia*) are easy to identify from their wavy-edged leaves. If yours is performing well get out there and remove the faded flowers and any dead or diseased stems. If the plant is a bit lacklustre, then removing one-third of the living stems from the base should pep it up.

H. arborescens (the most common of these is the cultivar 'Annabelle') has much thinner, floppier, smoother leaves and big, lollipop-like blooms which start off green, become white and then turn green again (see illustration, right). For pruning, see *H. paniculata*.

H. paniculata has smaller leaves that grow three to a
stem, in a whorl. Blooms come in a variety of different
shapes but always start off white and fade to dusty pink
with time. Both *H. arborescens* and *H. paniculata* bloom
on new wood, so if the shape bothers you, then
now is the time to correct things, removing any
wayward stems, or pruning to a framework,
just above a pair of buds, before the plant
starts galloping away with the warmer
weather of the spring.

Climbing hydrangeas can be left
well alone until after flowering.

NURTURE

....

Re-pot containers

If it's not too cold (for your fingers) then get ahead with some re-potting. Once permanent container plantings have outgrown their homes, they'll need to go a size up. If you're unsure, just remove the thing from its pot and look at the roots; if they are manifold and swirling around the edges of the compost then it's time to re-pot. The shopping expedition to find something suitable will take far more time than the actual re-potting, but when you have the vessel, simply fill to the right level with new compost and tease some of the roots of the plant away from its previous swirling pot formation, planting it gently in its new home with plenty of compost tucked around the sides. Water in well and feel good.

Harden off cuttings and seedlings

This is very much weather-dependent and needs your common sense rather than my words, but essentially you must determine whether it is time to start hardening off any cuttings or seedlings you have been storing indoors. Obviously don't do it if it's snowing and blowing a gale, but if the weather is clement, put your little ones in a clear plastic storage box (or cold-frame if you have one) with a lid, and place them outside with the lid on for a few days, bringing the whole thing in at night. Continue like this, cautiously, removing the lid when you feel it's right, until they are happy outside with the lid off. I would be unwilling to take them out of the box until April is out of the way, just in case of bad weather; if they're in a box, then it's easy as pie to bring them indoors if the weather suddenly turns nasty again.

Propagating *Pilea peperomioides*

Is your *Pilea* having babies? If so, then it's easy to get new plants by rooting the little ones in some water – no compost involved. If you don't own a *Pilea*, then this might just be the perfect time to treat yourself.

Here's how to propagate those babies:

Simply remove the plant from its pot. You'll see the babies around the edge of the pot.

Remove some of the soil so you get a good view of the small plants, and, using a clean sharp knife or a good pair of scissors, slice the babies off their mother, cutting a few centimetres below the lowest leaves.

Use a narrow-necked glass vase, or bottle, filled with water and balance the baby with the end of the stem just submerged in the water.

Give it a few weeks and you'll start to see new roots. It really is the loveliest way to discover propagation, on this most forgiving of houseplants.*

Dahlia beginnings

Have you got dahlia tubers? Put them in a tray with some compost and sprinkle some water on top to tell them it's time to wake up.

Sow some stuff, but curb your enthusiasm

If you have a greenhouse, then perhaps you have started sowing in earnest already. As someone without a greenhouse who values her sanity, I'm not a fan of sowing with reckless abandon, and certainly not in March. I prefer to wait a few weeks and sow in April to be sure my seedlings do not languish lankily indoors in the event of bad weather. It took me a long time to get to this stage, eagerly sowing seed by the packet as early as possible, only to run out of space on my window-sill when it came to potting on, or to lose most of my babies to bad weather because I had planted them out too early. Don't fret though; there are some plants I always sow early (sometimes in February if I'm feeling super-keen) – find some suggestions on page 17.

My favourite fast climbers

I know gardeners are supposed to play the long game, but it's okay to want a quick fix sometimes, especially for an empty wall or arbour. Here are the best quick climbers:

> **Honeysuckle:** a really good option for most sites, including shady ones. Think woodland and make sure its feet are firmly rooted in nice shady dampness (mulch please), and it will climb towards the light. *Lonicera periclymenum* 'Graham Thomas' is the classic, sweetly scented and beloved of birds, bees and butterflies, but if you need evergreen then plump

for *L. japonica* 'Halliana', which has the prettiest leaves
and an equally delicious scent.

Campsis radicans: a rather more unexpected beauty.
It climbs and sustains itself using aerial roots and
will cover anything as long as it gets good, moist,
well-drained soil and a sunny sight. An added bonus
are the lovely long seedpods it produces after flowering.

Climbing hydrangea (*Hydrangea anomala* subsp.
petiolaris): is deciduous and has the benefit of looking
fabulously posh. It will go great guns and cover a huge
area, and is self-clinging provided you give it adequate
water and the support is roughly textured.

English ivy: dense, smart, wildlife-rich cover that is
evergreen to boot, and all without the slightest effort
on your part. The golden rule with all of the above is
to give them the very best start, and that means taking
extra time to make sure the plants are really well
watered in, over a long period, and that they are
mulched annually.

A word on sowing seed and planting outside

Is it warm yet? Could you sit on the soil with your bare bottom
and not shriek? There's a chance it could be, but if that's the
case please don't get carried away with sowing and planting out
madly, because statistically it's more likely to snow at this time
of year than it is at Christmas, so the safe thing to do is to hang
tight and wait until next month, or even until May when you're
dealing with baby or young plants, just to be on the safe side.
On the other hand, this March might be the beginning of
summer, and you might take a gamble and win. Every March
is different. Your call.

Plants to cover ugly legs

There's no doubt about it, there are some plants for whom beauty up top is not shared down below. Lilies are one such unfortunate, with those awkward, skinny, hairy legs. Roses are another. Luckily there is lots of good hosiery out there for these poor loves, and nobody need ever know. Here are some suggestions for your shopping list.

Generally speaking, one is looking for thigh-high leg-warmers rather than ankle socks, so don't be confined to ground-cover because it won't cover enough up. And waft. Waft is essential, so that the stems can recede, and the good parts can be spied. *Nepeta*, lavender and *Salvia* are the three graces here, doing exactly the right amount of covering up and waving about, with the added benefit of acting as anti-fungal companion plants for susceptible roses. *Astrantia major*, *Artemisia*, *Gaura lindheimeri*, *Lychnis coronaria* and geranium get the job done too, adding to, rather than drowning out the main event. For an instant solution, why not try *Euphorbia* 'Diamond Frost' whose dancing smart foliage and white, frothy flowers are beloved of garden designers and nurserymen who use it to cover up a multitude of sins in the lower planting storeys. Finally, try *Pelargonium* 'Attar of Roses' for the perfect scented seasonal modesty defender.

FUSS

Sieve some compost

Some of the loveliest occupations are totally mindless, and this is one of them. If you have a store of pre-sieved compost you will love yourself forever, and your seeds will love you even more. In order to germinate successfully, seeds need relatively fine compost, so that their tiny, hair-like roots can navigate downwards and outwards to find water, nutrients and air and feed the plant. Sieving your compost gets rid of any large lumps that might impede this process, and also makes it easy for the seedling to emerge above the surface of the compost. All in all, then, sieved compost is a jolly good idea. Prepare a large, clean container and use multi-purpose, peat-free compost. Use a garden sieve, put something good on the headphones and sieve the whole lot into the container, like panning for gold, only discarding the nuggets of earth that are too large to fit through the holes.

Hedgehog house

Do you have one? If you don't have a hedgehog house in your outside space, then consider getting one – not just because hedgehogs are the cutest, but also because they are seriously in decline and need some help from us. Check out proprietary hedgehog houses or make your own, but more importantly keep an area of your garden un-disturbed and un-tidied – this is good for all wildlife.

Bee hotels

Yes, those tiny houses crammed with bamboo canes and the like do actually work if you site them correctly. What is more, they look rather fabulous too, especially when hung up *en masse*. It's as easy as banging a nail into your trellis or wall, and the bees, on whom we all depend will thank you for it.

Project: Alpine strawberries

Don't be fooled by the fact that these are such a delicacy
– they are dead easy to grow from seed. You need:

· a packet of Alpine strawberry seeds
· a plug tray with lid filled with sieved multi-purpose
  compost, mixed with one third perlite
· more perlite to cover

Make sure the compost is damp by soaking the whole
  tray in another tray of water for a couple of hours.
Simply sprinkle the tiniest pinch of seed into each plug.
  These seeds are minuscule so don't even attempt to
  separate them out ... you'll do that when you thin them.
Cover with a thin layer of perlite and then put the whole
  thing in a warm bright place, with
  the lid on.

**When you notice tiny
  green leaves** suddenly
  appear in most of
  the plugs, take the
  lid off and keep the
  babies watered by
  misting the surface
  of the compost every
  now and then.

Gradually acclimatize the tray to the outside air
temperatures, using the hardening-off method on
page 42, until the thing is sitting outside happily, day
and night. Remember these are alpine plants and
therefore hardy.

Thin them out when they are a couple of centimetres tall
by ruthlessly snipping all but two or three seedlings at
their base with a pair of nail scissors (see my lowdown
on thinning, page 64).

Finally, remove each plug and separate the tiny seedlings
very carefully, planting two or three, equidistantly, into a
5cm (2in) pot at first, and then eventually into their own
pot, before you plant them out in the garden.

Yes, this is a 'project', but Alpine strawberries for pudding
are worth it.

April

'Every spring is the only spring:
a perpetual astonishment.'
Ellis Peters

It can be beastly yes, but we are almost there; it's the
end of winter and we're coming out the other side.

SPRUCE

If you haven't already begun, it's time to start feeding your
houseplants. Just a little bit mind ... you don't want to give
them gout. Choose a liquid feed that suits you and follow the
instructions to the letter. Feeding plants really does make a
huge difference, and if an indoor jungle is what you're after
then this is a good train to board.

Weeding games

Okay. The weeding, if you've only just stepped out into the garden after a long winter, is going to be intense for a while. The best, and least overwhelming way to approach it is via the square metre or 'hula-hoop' method (see page 172). Five minutes a day, one area. Go, go, go!

Re-potting and more

For permanent plantings, check to see if the plants need re-potting but more importantly, start to dream a little about what you're going to do with your containers this year. Perhaps you've already ordered some bedding, or possibly you want to wait until you can go to the garden centre and choose the things that take your fancy. Bear in mind that your five-minute garden will be so much easier if you stick to one or two plants in your containers. See pages 54–55 for my suggestions of container beauties that will provide you with a long season of interest and minimal upkeep. And don't forget those ferns (see page 29).

Re-potting houseplants

Just as with those outside, re-potting houseplants can also happen at this time of year as the light levels are going up and plants are waking up slowly. Simply tip the plant out of its existing pot to determine whether it needs a change of vessel (the signs of a pot being too tight for its occupant are roots running around the perimeter in mad circles). Remember that most houseplants need really great drainage; this is the single most important thing when it comes to keeping them happy. Whether they hail from the desert or the rainforest, they need a light mixture, to ensure that their roots never sit in water. To this end, I've found that ordinary, peat-free, multi-purpose compost, mixed half and half with perlite or grit is the best solution. Tuck your friend back into its new home and dampen the new compost, so that the roots of the plant know it's time to spread out.

Container plants, the five-minute way

Green is great: take a look at my suggestions for less ubiquitous containerised green beauty on pages 28–29, and obviously it's fine to add topiary, in the form of box or yew, to that list.

Lavender: healthy lavender in a terracotta pot (or indeed in profusion in the ground) is one of the more joyful things in life. Emphasis though, must be made on 'healthy'. Lavender plants are everywhere right now; soft and hummocky and about to burst, washing your summer garden in a glorious, buzzing purple haze. The reality, of course, is that lavender often becomes a casualty of its own allure in those early days. Bought on a whim and plonked somewhere unsuitable, it may flower for the summer, but will flounder eventually over a cold wet winter. Avoiding this depends very much on the type of soil in which it lives: the ground must be gritty and free-draining (think Mediterranean hillside), rather than cloddish and muddy where it will simply rot. Ensure then, that you add plenty of grit to the existing soil if necessary so that the roots never get properly wet. If you are planting a lavender hedge, then it's worth raising the ground and planting it on a ridge so that any lingering water drains away

quickly. See pruning tips on page 73 and page 104
and remember to keep the compost gritty.

Bedding: by which I mean tender plants grown
specifically for a season – and sold to you as either
plugs early in the year, or as larger plants. See my list of
favourite bedding on pages 29–30 and keep your choice
edited; a maximum of two different plants in profusion
is more cohesive than a different thing in each pot.

Summer bulbs: every year I order a monstrous quantity
of *Gladiolus callianthus* (scented, white, lily-like things
with a deep purple blotch in the middle) and they form
the backbone of my containers over the summer and
autumn. They can also be put in the ground, filling in all
the little gaps that may be nagging at you. In short, they
are a very good thing, and if you don't have any yet, then
I'd urge you to get some, and stagger their planting,
putting some in now, and another lot in at the end of
May, which will give you flowers all the way through until
the end of October. Gladiolus are not the only summer
bulbs though. Lilies, *Crocosmia*, *Kniphofia* and nerines
are all worth having as long as you can give them the
right conditions.

Perennial pot queens: see my list of the hardest working
perennials for pots on page 59.

CHOP

········

Lawn stuff

Eek! Could it be time to give the lawn its first mow? If so then set the mower to a high setting. While you're at it, consider some lawn resolutions that you might factor into your five-minute bursts this year.

Mowing every week, once you've got the lawn to a height you like, will reduce your workload considerably, and you won't have to use the clipping bucket. Just let the clippings fall as you mow and fertilise it. Job done.

Edging is essential for that calm feeling. A mown lawn without a crisp edge is a trick missed and I urge you to try it if you don't do it already. In fact, if you can't be bothered to mow, then just edging will keep things feeling slightly under control.

Aerating: get some aerating sandals and flounce about in them to aerate the sward. This will allow water and nutrients to get into the grass roots and your lawn will love you for it.

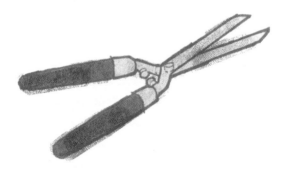

Scarifying: take a spring tine rake and lightly drag it over the lawn to remove dead grass (thatch) and anything else that may be lurking. This is best done in autumn, because it generally makes things look rather horrid for a bit, and you don't want that when you're about to use your lawn the most, but you can also do a bit now, if you have a bad thatch problem. Remember to set some thatch aside – it makes the best kindling for fires.

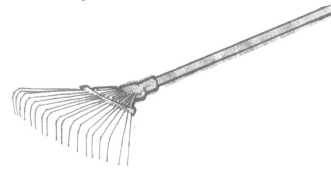

Leave some of it to grow long. Honestly, leaving part of my lawn alone between May or June and October was one of the best decisions I ever made. It massively increased the wildlife in my garden and obviously cut down my workload at the same time. You can also plant bulbs in an unmown lawn which will come up to delight you in the spring. The only thing not to like is that the rough area will remain forever that – rough, with the odd gap where the light fails to get in over the summer. If that is going to fry your brain then don't do it, but otherwise there is *nothing* not good about having a mini meadow.

Pick your tulips

I have a bit of a mania when it comes to things I can pick, which means that I prefer vases chock-full of tulips than a garden dotted with them. That's just my personal preference, but you don't need to pick every last one ... in fact, just one tulip, by the bed, is the most glorious of things. Remember that by cutting these, you are also basically deadheading them too, and that means that they're more likely to grow well the following year ... just a thought.

NURTURE

·······································

Best perennials for pots

The right perennials, growing in a pot are a five-minute gardener's dream. They don't need fussing or faffing with, like bedding, and they certainly don't need replacing year after year. Here are my favourites:

Erigeron karvinskianus (Mexican daisy): if there's one plant I would recommend to a beginner gardener with a garden of ANY size, it would be this one. It will bloom for longer than any other thing in the garden, and it will seed everywhere; in cracks and crevices, on walls, between steps – to soften and lift any space.

Alchemilla mollis: indestructible and SO pretty, even over winter. Best, freshest green in town with the addition of acid green flowers.

Heuchera: people are stuffy about heucheras, but they look really beautiful in containers, particularly the purple ones. Really low-maintenance and textural.

Myosotis: you cannot beat a forget-me-not in a pot. Unsurpassed glory. Thrives on neglect. Not even going to say anything else.

Plant out forced bulbs

If you have any hyacinths languishing indoors after their winter wondrousness, why not plant them outside rather than throwing them away? If I had planted all the bulbs I ever bought for indoor decoration I'd have a garden to rival any Dutch field by now. Pick a spot and resolve to plant all of them in one area every year from now on.

Dahlia shoot watch

You'll probably be able to see some shoots on your dahlias by now. If so, you can pot them into old plastic pots of an appropriate size, making sure they're the right way up (the tubers should be 'drooping' downwards).

Herbs

Do you have any herbs? If not, they are the five-minute gardener's dream, being both beautiful and useful. Here's how to have them all with the minimum of effort. This is the one area where it's cool to have small pots!

Have bay, rosemary and sage in the ground. If you can't do that, then put them all in one pot with John Innes No 2 compost and lots of grit.

Have mint in its own pot, multi-purpose compost.

Have oregano in its own pot, multi-purpose compost with grit.

Have thyme in its own pot, multi-purpose compost with grit.

Have parsley in its own pot, multi-purpose compost with
   John Innes No. 2 and feed weekly.
Coriander is easiest grown as a microgreen (see page 19).

And the most important thing with all of these (with the
exception of bay which will grow into a tree if you let it) is
to harvest regularly, which will keep the plant in shape.

Plant out sweet peas

Hurrah! If you sowed some in autumn then well done you! They
should be ready to plant out now, as long as it's not snowing and
blowing a gale. If you didn't, then you can still sow now for your
sweet pea fix (see page 131), or don't stress it and just buy some
seedlings ready-grown.

Prepare the ground by digging holes or a trench for your plants,
and lining the bottom with a mixture of well-rotted manure and
compost. Take enormous care when freeing your sweet peas from
their nursery pots, as they don't like root disturbance, and make
sure you give them something to climb up. Tuck them in tight
and water well.

Cuttings

Have you taken any yet? If not, it's really easy and a fabulous way to feel accomplished and clever. See pages 76–77.

Easy annuals to direct sow

As long as the weather is nice, and you can go outside without a coat, neck exposed, and as long as it's been like that for a good ten days, then you can think about sowing some seed outside. The lovely thing about direct sowing is that there's no transplanting of seed or hardening off required. The not-so-lovely thing is that your seedlings can lie prone to slugs, snails, birds, cats, rabbits, mice and the rest, who like to eat the babies or scratch around in the earth and mess up your life. That's okay. The plants are worth the effort. See pages 130–132 for the how-to and try *Ammi majus*, cornflower and calendula if it's your first time. You're going to need to be very vigilant and remove as many slugs and snails as you can on your travels around the garden (see slug and snail defences, page 84). You can also use thorny prunings, laid over the sown area, to keep animals and birds away.

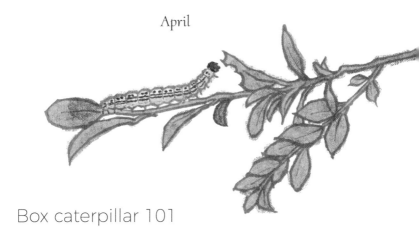

Box caterpillar 101

Cydalima perspectalis is the box tree caterpillar. It lays pale yellow eggs on the underside of the leaves, which hatch green and yellow caterpillars with black heads. These will munch away, leaving only crispy brown skeletons of leaves, and making you both angry and sad. At the time of writing, this gardener has had success with a mixture of vigilance, moth traps and a spray called 'Xentari' which is not on the British market yet. Hand removal is disgusting but effective – anything is better than using chemical sprays which kill the moths and every other beneficial insect. The ultimate solution is to use something other than box. Here are my top three box replacements:

Yew: beautiful, clippable, indestructible; I love it.
Sarcococca confusa: a bit more relaxed than box and not as clippable, but oh my, the winter scent more than makes up for that – see page 14.
Lonicera nitida: sometimes called poor man's box – the clue is in the name.

Thinning out: the rules

Thinning seedlings out can be gut-wrenching – it's awful to do away with perfectly good seedlings but it is one of the most important parts of raising from seed; your plants will never reach their full potential if you aren't ruthless about giving them the space they need to grow. Here are the rules:

Sow thinly in the first place; less is more.

Sow in modules or tiny pots. Sowing in pairs is a good option as it will give you an insurance policy. When both seedlings come up, wait until they are 2.5cm (1in) high and snip the smaller one off at soil level. If your seeds are too small to sow singly, snip all but one or two seedlings away in each module. Two seedlings, in either corner of a small module can then grow on for a while and eventually one can be pricked out and transplanted, avoiding wastage.

In the ground, sow thinly as before and when the seedlings are 2–3cm (1in) tall, do an initial thinning by leaving one good seedling every 10cm (4in) and pulling everything out in between. Watering before you remove seedlings will avoid root damage to neighbours, and watering post-thinning is essential too, to settle the compost around the roots. A second thinning (to whatever the packet instructs) can then ensue, when you feel the plants are strong enough to withstand transplanting. At this stage, the removed plants can be replanted elsewhere.

FUSS

Bend climbing roses downwards

If you have climbing roses then now is the perfect time to spend five minutes tying-in their still-soft stems to whatever they're climbing up against. If you bend the stems downwards you'll be encouraging more flowers too.

Tie anything and everything in

... as it grows. The difference you can make to a garden by judiciously tying-in climbers and rambling things is immeasurable. Your eyesores will be covered from top to bottom, and your fences will look the business. It's one of those things that is easy if you do it every day and impossible to do once the horse has bolted.

Start deadheading and don't stop

Another trick of the trade – people with extremely floriferous gardens are those who go out daily with their scissors. The more going-over flowers you chop, the more new and beauteous flowers your plants will produce. Simple. Go nowhere without your scissors.

Staking 101

The network of support used to produce the amazing results we see in some grand herbaceous borders requires an unattainable level of work for us ordinary mortals. Happily, there are a range of rather less-exhausting alternatives. We should all stake our plants before they have need of staking. I'm old enough to know that this hardly ever happens though; staking for me is most often a five-minute, reactive dash to save a plant from snapping.

- **Very tall plants,** like sunflowers, can be tied to a cane or pea stick driven deep into the ground to keep them sturdy. There are the bought options – a single metal pole with a curly bit at the top that you can drive into the ground, which does the same thing as a bamboo cane without the need for string.
- **For shorter plants** that have a tendency to flop there are metal supports – basically mini 'fences', which you push into the soil for the plant to lean on. There are also dome-like structures you can buy for plants to grow through. Pliable hazel or willow sticks are great for this if you fancy having a go yourself.
- **For everything,** the very best method I have found is twiggy branches of all sizes pushed in around each plant or just in front of them, which recede obligingly from a distance, and look lovely close-up.

Project: Moving big stuff

Niggling feelings along the lines of 'That huge bush would just look so much better over there' are best acted on this month. Garner some help, make a plan and move anything large now to a new, better home. You can spend your life faffing around with tiny details, and they do count, but of course it's the big changes that are transformational. Bite the bullet.

Mulching

If you didn't manage to mulch in the autumn or winter months, then think about putting some well-rotted manure at the bases of all your shrubs and trees now, as the soil is warming up. It's understandably difficult to mulch when you've got lots of pretty bulbs in the borders, so just do some targeted mulching, five minutes at a time, with a trowel and a trug of muck (see pages 154–156). You can keep on doing this throughout the year; the only rule is that the ground is neither too dry, nor too cold, so water, or wait accordingly.

Alpine landscapes

Alpines are both beautiful and tough. A wide shallow pot of a
few of these amazing plants is one of the loveliest adornments
for any outdoor table.

You need a wide, shallow container – terracotta is great, or you
could get a trough made of tufa, which looks like rock. Throw
some crocks in the bottom for really good drainage, and fill
with some very gritty compost (I use multi-purpose in a 50/50
mix with horticultural grit). Next, plant your Alpines – a
mixture of different colours, shapes and textures works best.
You can plant them quite close together – these plants tend to
creep slowly. I love alpine dianthus, irises and all manner of
saxifrages, but there are no rules here. Things can get really
interesting if you use shards of slate or bits of broken pot set
vertically in the container in the manner of a craggy hillside,
and fill these with more compost, squishing the plants into
these small gaps. Once everything is in, simply mulch with
pea-gravel, water, and then put the container somewhere
you can see it easily and gawp shamelessly.

May

*'Spring is nature's way of saying
"Let's party".'*
Robin Williams

SPRUCE

Weeding, watering and wondering

If you have no time to do anything else in the garden this
month, then the above activities will suffice. Pulling weeds as
and when you see them, and watering your containers and any
newly planted specimens regularly to give them the very best
start in life are the key to keeping your garden and its most
important inhabitant (you) happy. These endeavours will
naturally comprise what I would sum up as a 'daily mooch',
which will do more for your garden than reading any books
or consulting any oracles – it will breed familiarity. Your
gardening can then become purely reactive – which is fine –
you'll see something that needs doing, and either dash off
to achieve it, or put it on your mental list for tomorrow.

Setting up

It's vital, at this time of year, to remember what your garden is for. For me, that means going out into it and enjoying it with my family – but that will never happen if I don't make it easy for myself. To this end, around this time of year I put cushions on chairs, and raise a parasol or two every morning. It takes 30 seconds and is a simple way to ensure that when I snag that precious five minutes for a cup of tea (or a glass of something) then I can sit down comfortably and feel like a queen. Try it; this simple act of stage-setting will transform the way you use your garden, and thus have it serve its intended purpose.

Sweeping

Paths and terraces will always benefit from regular sweeping, even though there may not be much in the way of detritus. It prevents build-up of weed seeds in little cracks and crevices and, most importantly, creates an inviting environment for you to enjoy.

CHOP

Prune early-flowering clematis

These beauties will have finished flowering by now, so take off any bits you don't like or that have gone astray. For other clematis, see page 25.

The Chelsea chop

The garden may look glorious and abundant, and it's tempting to let her lounge, but if you can bear to fly around wielding something sharp before high summer hits, then she will reap the benefits of extended youth and vigour, at least for the rest of the season. The theory is simple: plants want to flower and set seed in order to produce the next generation. If that process is interrupted by you and your secateurs, then most of them will have another go at flowering while the weather is still on side.

There's no blanket rule you can apply regarding when and what to chop; it requires a bit of nosing around in the undergrowth and some common sense. By chopping I mean yanking, pruning, pinching and clipping – all of which come under the guise of general tidying as and when the mood arises. I shall be twisting and pulling out the flowers of *Alchemilla mollis*, cutting back *Geranium phaeum* (the ones which show new growth at the crown). I will be chopping *Nepeta*, thyme and *Santolina* back by at least half, and doing the same to some of my more out-of-control lavender. If I'm feeling super-organised I'll be cutting back some of my late-summer-blooming plants to remove any possibility of them getting floppy and falling over. Good aftercare (regular watering) is a must for any plant that has just had surgery; a small price to pay for beauty regained and pleasure prolonged.

Lawn love

You can start mowing with a bit more gusto now that the grass has really started growing. Always remember that edging is the finishing touch that will really lift your lawn, and if you don't already have a pair, it's worth investing in some proper edging shears for this.

NURTURE

Container-garden secrets

All those growers you see at flower shows have some very simple tricks to create the amazing displays you think you'll never achieve. Here they are.

They water their plants, like, reguarly. See my tips on watering on page 83.

They feed their plants, regularly. Put a schedule in your phone and make it ping, bing or chirp at you every couple of weeks so you don't forget to feed your containers.

They deadhead their plants regularly. See pages 86–87 for my deadheading tips.

And that's it. If you follow those three golden rules, you'll have erupting containers of love just like them.

A meadow of sorts

Consider creating a bit of meadow in your lawn round about now. It really doesn't have to be huge – just a square metre (11 sq. ft) will do. It will add interest and texture to the overall look of your garden, and provide insects with an undisturbed habitat, which in turn means that you are helping the birds and generally contributing to the biodiversity of your space. Oh, and it will cut your mowing time considerably. I'd call that a win-win. Here's the 101 if you're interested:

Get the grass to 5cm (2in) in height, removing and composting any mowings, and then leave it alone from late May onwards for the summer. It's not a wildflower meadow by any stretch, but it will provide a mini jungle for all sorts of wildlife and add interest to your lawn.

As long as you cut the short bits with panache, creating clean lines and a stark contrast between long and short, then it will look intentional, and therefore a feast for the eyes. Mowing around the edge of a lawn and leaving the centre long is a great first step, but sweeping paths, mazes or geometric designs are all possible with a little forethought. If the long-grass thing works for you then consider replacing with soil-appropriate wildflower meadow, which can be bought by the roll or as seed mixes.

Peony love

Oh, my goodness – do you have peonies? If you do, why aren't you picking them so you can put them by your bed? If you don't have peonies, then perhaps you should think about getting some. They're the most obliging things that like a bit of shade and some nice rich soil, but are otherwise undemanding, despite the fact that they look like the floral equivalent of a film star. Order now to avoid disappointment.

Taking softwood cuttings

Great news! You can take cuttings of all the plants you need gazillions of but can't afford (think hydrangea, *Philadelphus*, lavender, *Penstemon*, *Pelargonium*, *Verbena bonariensis* ... I could go on). Each needs slightly different treatment, but the general idea is the same.

May

You need really sharp secateurs, a knife or scalpel, containers and cuttings compost (I use a mixture of pearlite, vermiculite, sand and bought cuttings compost). Most importantly, everything should be scrupulously clean.

Water your parent plant the night before, and snip the next morning just below a pair of leaves, preferably on a non-flowering shoot, leaving two to three pairs of leaves above. Remove the tip from the cutting, just above a pair of leaves, to encourage bushiness, and also remove the lowest pair with a sharp knife. You should be left with a 5–10cm (2–4in) cutting, with one pair of leaves. If the leaves are big, as with hydrangea, slice them in half to reduce moisture loss. Make a hole in the compost with a pencil, push the cutting in so that the leaves sit just above the surface, and firm gently around each one. Repeat around the side of the pot (cuttings seem to like company), water thoroughly and place in a propagator or put a large sandwich bag over the pot, sealing with an elastic band.

Keep cuttings on your kitchen window-sill where you can check on them, making sure the compost is moist but not wet, and your new plants should root within a few weeks, at which point they can be potted on and hardened off outside, ready for planting in the garden.

Planting new things

The thrill of putting something new into the ground never gets old. Here is how to plant properly and ensure that anything you plant has the best start in life:

Dig a hole roughly twice the size of the plant you want to put in it. The reason for this is to decompact the soil and make it easy for the roots of the plant to spread out.

Water the plant properly before you put it in the ground. Why? Because if you put a desiccated plant into the ground and water it, then it will stay dry and not thrive.

Put manure, or grit in the bottom of the planting hole (according to the plant's needs) and mix it a bit with the existing soil. Manure will provide food for hungry plants, and grit will provide drainage for ones that don't like wet feet.

Muss the roots of the plant about a bit before you plant. This will let the roots know that it's okay to explore.

After planting, create a wall around the newly planted specimen by pushing some soil up all around it. When you water the plant, this wall will keep the water where it's needed.

Most importantly, water your plant in properly. A thorough, long dousing is infinitely preferable to a bit here and there. You want to encourage the roots down towards the water table, so that the plant can eventually look after itself. If the roots stay on the surface in response to little-and-often watering, then you're sentencing yourself to a lifetime of watering.

Dahlia things

If your dahlias have two or three pairs of leaves, then you can go in and pinch off the 'leading shoot' at its base. The leading shoot is the one in the middle, reaching for the sky. Removing it will encourage lots of sideshoots, and that means more flowers. Also, have you decided where your dahlias will go? Prepare the ground by sprinkling it with blood, fish and bone, raking it in, and adding stakes where each plant is going to grow. If they're going in large pots, mix some of this in with the compost and, again, add a stake or three. Whatever you do, have it ready for planting your babies at the end of this month, at which time you should dig a big hole for each plant and fill the bottom of it with well-rotted manure. Once they are in, tie the plants gently to the stake (see tying-in, page 118), water them well and wait.

Planting out your edibles

Is the weather lovely yet? If you've hardened off your tomato or chilli seedlings (or if you've just bought some from the shops) then it's time to plant them out. I love using a huge hanging basket for my tumbling tomatoes, and chillies go in smaller pots (a departure from my usual ways, because I like to bring them indoors over the winter). Hanging baskets need multi-purpose compost mixed with water-retaining granules to keep things damp. Mix the compost and water it before you do any planting, as these granules will expand, and you may well need to remove some of the compost. Plant seven tomatoes to a 45cm (17in) diameter hanging basket, angling the plants outwards, cover with more compost and hang up somewhere safe and sunny. Chillies can go in John Innes No. 2, where they will be very happy indeed.

Ready to sow something new?

How about some winter squash and courgettes? Summer projects, though of course not strictly necessary, are nonetheless a welcome diversion, particularly if you have children to entertain, and sowing squash is a fail-safe exercise that will yield fantastic results fast. First, buy some seeds; I love growing weird, wonderful, warty winter squash, which are food for the eye as well as the stomach, with the added bonus of maturing into rock-hard bauble-type-things, which you can pile in a bowl and gaze at all winter. They are also very useful for suppressing weeds if you have a bare space to fill. These plants grow really big and will need something to climb up, unless you're okay with them trailing around on the ground. Sow only as many as you can accommodate – each one needs a 50cm (20in)-plus container or a square metre (11 sq. ft) of earth.

Start them off in small pots inside your kitchen by the window.

Sow one seed to a pot, vertically on its side about 1cm (⅜in) deep.

Once germinated, grow on until you have a strong little seedling, and then start hardening off (see page 42) until ready to plant out (roots filling the pot; healthy happy baby plant).

If you're using a container, make it as large as possible, and fill with multi-purpose compost. A sunny site is optimal, and watering is crucial. Start feeding once a fortnight as soon as flowers appear.

A climbing frame in the form of a pergola or tepee is important here, but other than that they really only need watering and feeding – easy five-minute endeavours and massive payback; to say these things are impressive would be an understatement.

Salad

There's no such thing as a five-minute veg patch. Sorry, there just isn't. A productive veg patch is one of life's labour-intensive things. But that doesn't mean you can't have your cake and eat it. Cut-and-come-again salad is an easy solution and will keep you in greens from May until September and beyond. You need:

- a packet of mixed leaves
- two wide shallow containers filled with multi-purpose compost.

Water one container and at this point set a reminder on your phone to sow the other pot in two weeks' time.

Sprinkle a pinch of seeds evenly over the surface of the watered compost and cover lightly with some sieved compost. Jam a bamboo cloche over the top of the pot, just to keep naughty children, squirrels and other beasties away from this inviting pot of nothing but dirt.

Within a few weeks you'll have leaves to pick; pluck them individually as and when you need them. The second pot of leaves will take over from the first once it is exhausted, at which point you can clear whatever remains and start again when your phone reminds you.

Repeat the fortnightly sowing cycle until the weather closes in. If you love your salads, double up on your pots.

FUSS

Watering regimes

If you can make watering your containers like brushing your teeth (I HOPE you brush your teeth), then the whole thing will become a breeze. Here, for what it's worth, is how I manage it. I own a lot of watering cans and an old-fashioned tin 'bath', which I keep full of water at all times from a hosepipe. This bath is the key to saving time as I fill the watering cans from it (just dunking; no waiting), and once I've watered my containers I fill the cans again, so that they are ready to go for the next time. If your garden is purely containers (or if you are so inclined) then an irrigation system is well worth the time and effort it takes to set up. If you are someone who has a brain that can work out timers, then this is even better. In the ground, my rule is that except in the most sweltering heat, if  something needs watering regularly, then it probably shouldn't be there. See planting tips on page 78 for why this is the case.

Houseplant love

Keep wiping the dust off any leaves indoors, and keep watering and feeding as per your regime.

Slug and snail defences

Most of the fussing this month and beyond is going to revolve around slimy invertebrates, and ensuring that they understand the concept of SHARING. Whenever you see a slug or a snail pick it up and put it in a jar or pot or whatever. 'Dispose' of them however you and your conscience sees fit, but personally I like to release them somewhere else, far away, like my local park. I put the jar down under a bush and by the time I come back from picking up the kids, they have all dispersed. This is the easiest option, but if you can't face touching them, here are some other ways and means of keeping your population 'balanced':

Copper bands around pots; they won't cross the band.
Vaseline around pots; again, they won't cross a Vaselined area but you will need to top it up.
Crushed-up eggshells around prized plants – needs constant upkeep and a LOT of eggshells, but if you get through a lot of eggs then this is a useful endeavour and a good way of composting. Dry the eggshells out in a low oven first to make them easier to crush.
Beer traps (although anecdotal evidence suggests that slugs wait for their friends to drown and then use them as sacrificial bridges). Bury a small container full of beer at soil level and let them fall in.
Nematodes for slugs, which are effective as long as instructions are followed to the letter.

Water for the birds

If you have a pond or pool, then cool, but if not, then adding a simple bowl of water anywhere away from human traffic for the birds to drink from is a very good thing.

Keep thinning your seedlings

It's so important (see pages 64–65).

Be ready with string

For tying-in ... see page 118 and replenish your stocks if they are running low.

Start hardening things off

You may indeed have already started acclimatising some of your baby or tender plants to outdoor temperatures, but I'm writing this book with the memory of the 'Beast From the East' of 2018 still fresh in my traumatised mind. There was persistent snow all the way into May, so forgive me if I'm a little cautious. You can see my tips on hardening off seedlings on page 42, but I'm speaking here of dahlias, cannas and the like, which you may be bringing into life indoors (shed or garage) and are now ready for a bit of reality. First, open the doors and windows in the daytime for a few days, and then put the pots outside in the daytime for a week. After that, if the weather forecast is okay, then leave them outside overnight.

Top dressing containers

If you have containers with permanent plantings in them, you can help them along by removing the top 5cm (2in) of soil and replacing it with new. This will provide the plant with added nutrients and make the whole thing look rather gorgeous too.

Project: Garlic pest spray

It's not proven but garlic is an anecdotal winner when it comes to deterring pests from emerging soft sappy growth, so if you have problems with insects eating your veg or flowers, but don't want to use toxic pesticides, try a homemade concoction by blending up three garlic bulbs (separated into cloves but skin included) with a cup of water. Add this to two pints of water and a squirt of eco washing-up liquid, strain through a cheesecloth and dilute with ten parts water to use.

Deadheading – the whys and hows

Although deadheading is as simple as removing spent flowers, there are a few tips that can help you to do it better and more efficiently. It's also useful to know the 101 on why we deadhead and it is this: a plant's entire *raison d'être* is to flower, set seed and reproduce itself. Flowers, then, are not there to make your life wonderful – that's just serendipity – no, flowers are there to attract pollinators so that they will come and help the plant in its grand plan. Once the flower fades, seed is made, and this takes a lot of energy. But if you come in and remove the flower before it has set seed, the plant will be spurred on to produce more of them. Add a feeding regime to help the plant out, and you have a continual display as the plant begins again to try to produce seed. To deadhead most plants, all that is needed is

your thumb and forefinger
and possibly help from your
thumbnail. Tougher plants,
like roses, will snap just
beneath the base of the
flower. Sometimes the
flowers are so tiny (*Nemesia*)
that you can go in with shears
and give the whole thing a haircut
all in one go. Or you can use nail
scissors and get properly obsessive about it.
Whatever you do, the idea behind it is the same. A lot of
summer pruning is actually just drastic deadheading (see
Chelsea chop, page 73). Importantly though, remember that
some plants actually look glorious in death, and you will want
the seedheads in your life to feed the birds and make your
garden gorgeous.

Outdoor chandeliers

Hanging baskets are a brilliant way to have floral profusion
without sacrificing space at ground level. My favourite (because
it's easy) is a basket full of trailing petunias. Begin with
multi-purpose compost mixed with water-retaining granules.
Fill the largest basket you can safely hang (because larger is key
when it comes to watering) and water first, with water laced
with tomato fertiliser, to allow the granules to expand. Now
plant petunia plugs around the edges and in the centre,
back-filling as you go. Put a reminder on your phone to feed
every couple of weeks and you'll have a bright pink cornucopian
vision before long. Remember that hanging baskets (and all
containers) need daily watering in the summer.

June

'What is one to say about June, the time of perfect young summer. The fulfilment of the promise of the earlier months, and with as yet no sign to remind one that its fresh young beauty will ever fade.'

Gertrude Jekyll

SPRUCE

Hoe, hoe, hoe!

Keep weeding in five-minute bursts, every day, for a hassle-free life. This doesn't necessarily mean getting down on your hands and knees (although that's where I usually end up). There are plenty of hoes with different-length handles out there for anyone dealing with mobility issues. Sunny weather is the perfect time to hoe – you just slice small seedlings with the hoe, below the soil, and leave the tops to frazzle on the surface in the sunshine; no clearing up needed.

Watering in general

Keep watering assiduously. See my planting rules on pages 78 but also take note of any new trees or shrubs that you planted in the autumn or winter and give these long, slow drenches during very dry weather. The best way to do this is to run the hose at a trickle and leave it at the base of the plant for 12 hours or so.

Setting up the garden

Your favourite chair. It needs to be out. Every day – unless torrential rain is forecast, so that your garden can fulfil its destiny. It matters. Cushions, throws, parasols, games and the rest should be easily accessible if they are not put out. Have a special space for them, right by the door to the garden.

CHOP

Mow

If you've decided to grow some of your lawn, then mowing should be reduced dramatically and only take a few moments, especially if you are doing it every week because you don't need to toss the clippings anywhere – they can go straight back on the lawn. If you don't have a lawn, then well done, you're living your best five-minute life.

Prune spring-flowering shrubs

All those beautiful shrubs that flowered for you over the spring months – such as forsythia (the yellow-flowered one) or *Philadelphus* (the white one with the delicious bubble-gum scent) or *Ribes* (the flowering currant, with cascading tendrils of little pink or white flowers) – can now be pruned if you so wish. Just find strong, young shoots lower down the plant and cut back to them. Remember that in general with pruning, less is more, and that you must consistently step back to consider the entire plant, rather than just the bit you are lopping off. Keep your secateurs clean as a whistle (see page 24) and cut up your prunings as you go to make tidying up a breeze and your compost heap happy.

Sweet peas

Are your sweet peas flowering yet? Make sure you pick them as soon as each flower emerges, and that you have a constant stream of little vases ready for the results of your labours. A house full of sweet peas is one of life's more glorious things and something to be fully proud of. Enjoy.

Stake

See my staking tips on page 67. If you've been amazing, and pre-staked everything in your garden, then hurrah! But if you are human, there will be rather a lot of reactive staking going on. Have your staking kit ready (see page 34), and as soon as you see something that looks like it might need support, stick a cane or twiggy branch in the appropriate place.

Observe your house guests

Take a look at your houseplants. It's okay. Life is busy and we all forget to water sometimes, especially cacti. If you find any shrivelled specimens languishing, then water them!

June

Box clipping

One of my favourite five-minute enterprises is to start clipping my box balls. Check first for box caterpillar (see page 63), and then go in with a pair of sharp shears, clipping cautiously but with confidence. Remember that random shapes are always more beautiful than perfect ones, and that in the end it is the quality of the clipping rather than the symmetry of the shape that makes topiary so alluring. See opposite for the 101 on topiary.

NURTURE

Divide snowdrops and bluebells

If you've got large clumps of these beauties then now is the time to lift them up and tease them apart before replanting, gently. This will help your collection to expand and avoid that crowded look; you want a sprinkling rather than a lump.

Squashes and courgettes

Have you been hardening off indoor-raised plants? If so it's time to plant them out now, either into huge containers

Project: Topiary clipping

If you're seeking the calm, laid-back feel that only clean lines can add to a garden, then a few clipped forms and a mown lawn will get you there faster than any amount of fussing about in the borders. Don't be constrained to box or yew; if you have a small-leaved evergreen in your garden that you think would look better clipped, then go for it. Don't be too rigid in your expectations either; allow the plant to dictate the finished form. A beautifully clipped blob will look better than something that's forced into a perfect geometric shape.

Your shears must be sharp – really sharp (see my tips on tool sharpening on page 24) – and the key to getting a tight shape is to tousle the foliage after every few snips. Go in with your hand and shake the branches and leaves. If you're baffled, go to YouTube and watch a professional clipping some box to see this technique in action. Keep standing back to observe your work and do it bit by bit – five-minute bursts are good!

Clipping should be done ideally on a dull, dry day to prevent the newly cut leaves scorching. In terms of post-clipping care, if the plant is happy and in the ground then you don't need to fertilise afterwards (container plants are a different matter and can be doused with liquid seaweed).

(see pages 80–81) or a square metre (11sq. ft) of prepared soil (and by 'prepared' I mean weed-free and beefed up with a few bucketfuls of well-rotted manure – that goes for containers too). Be really vigilant about slugs and snails (see page 84). If you didn't sow indoors but still want squash, then sow direct into the prepared soil. Poke two seeds into the centre of the patch, pushing them in 5cm (2in) deep, and protect with a makeshift, open-top cloche, cut out from a plastic bottle. Water well every day and as soon as you see action, cull the weaker seedling and watch the lucky one go.

Dahlia dalliances

Water your dahlias and be patient. They're going to sit there for a good few weeks doing not very much. Don't be fooled; they're just delaying your gratification. Water at the base of the plant and keep it up.

Summer holidays

At this time of year, you can start putting houseplants outside for their annual summer holidays. *Hippeastrums* (see pages 142–143), succulents and cacti (make sure they don't get rained on though), citrus trees if you have them, and the rest. See pages 106–107.

Sow some annuals

There's plenty of time still to sow some annuals if you feel like an affair with some seeds. See page 62 for my favourite easy annuals to direct sow, and remember that the key here, above all else, is the quality of your tilth and your level of vigilance against creatures who will want their fill of your little babies once they emerge.

FUSS

Deadheading

Glass of wine in one hand, thumb and forefinger at the ready with the other. Five minutes of fussing will keep flowers coming again and again. See page 86 for deadheading rules.

Feeding

Keep on dosing your containers with fertiliser – tomato fertiliser is the one you want here, as it promotes flowering. It really is the way to get amazing displays when it comes to summer displays like pelargoniums, petunias, lobelia, nemesias and the rest. These are either temporary displays, or they will be going back inside for the winter, so you don't need them to be tough. Feed them.

Equally, don't forget your tomatoes and chillies if you have them – do you see flowers yet? If it's a yes, then start feeding every week.

Tie in

Keep those bits of string handy (see page 34) and tie in new shoots as they emerge. Remember that your climbing plant doesn't actually care that you need it to cover your trellis evenly – all it knows is the insatiable desire to grow up, up, up, towards the light. It's your responsibility to guide it gently.

Grit is your friend

A bag of horticultural grit is one of my favourite things in the garden. You can use grit to mix with compost, of course, making it more free-draining, but grit can also be used to top dress pots with, reducing evaporation and therefore moisture loss, and making the whole thing look smart and chic. I also use grit to top dress all my indoor plants, as this keeps fruit flies at bay, and obviously helps to retain moisture. So, if you have potted plants without under-planting, take five minutes to put some grit around the base; you won't regret it.

Aphids 101

These things really are worth a bit of fussing about. Aphids are sap-suckers that, as long as there is balance in the garden, are perfectly harmless to most plants. But an infestation of them can be fatal, so check over the plants which aphids love to eat (I'm talking nasturtiums, marigolds, etc.) and if you see any, just squish them gently between your fingers (or wash them off with a jet of water). It's very much worth ordering some ladybirds, who will feast on your aphids happily, as long as they are strategically placed.

Vine weevils

Okay. These things are totally gross and need to be dealt with in the severest way possible. Here is the lowdown. The adults look like dark grey beetles and they munch leaves, but it's the babies that cause the damage. If a plant looks like it's wilting from lack of water, but doesn't respond when you douse it, then dig down a little to inspect the roots because you may find them – fat and white and revolting, munching away at the root system until there is very little left.

Obviously, if you see them, remove them and destroy them, replacing old soil with new and washing the roots for good measure. Chemical-free revenge is absolutely possible with nematodes, which allow you to pull out the big guns without any collateral damage (they are completely harmless to everything except vine-weevil grubs). A tiny weeny creature called *Steinernema kraussei* will help to keep things under control, and prevent further infestations. You simply add the nematodes to some water, and then water your plants. It's important to ensure that the soil is already moist, both to help the nematode move around, and prevent it from passing directly through the soil and out of the bottom of the pot. They will then work their way into the grubs and spew out blood-poisoning bacteria to nuke them from the inside. Lovely, just lovely.

July

*'People take pictures of the summer, just in
case someone thought they had missed it,
and to prove that it really existed.'*
Ray Davies

Look, it's summer, and I'm going to sound like a broken record,
but making sure there are cushions and umbrellas and lovely
places to sit in the garden is your number-one priority. For this
is, after all, the reason why we have an outdoor space.

My approach is to set the garden up in the morning,
whether I have plans to relax in it or not. If there is nowhere
to sit comfortably, then the chances of me relaxing in the
garden are zero, but if there is a comfortable chair with a pretty
cushion out there, waiting for me, then that probability goes up
by a mile. The simple process of putting out cushions in the
morning, and putting them away at night, a bit like making
your bed, becomes a rebellious act of self-respect when it
facilitates space-creation for just being. Try it.

Water-wise words

If you're suffering drought, then my condolences, and here are a few simple things that will help you to conserve water and make life easier.

First and foremost, try to install a water butt – no matter how small. It'll help – see page 119.

Avail yourself of a large container in which you can keep a supply of water and simply dunk your watering cans to fill them up (see page 83).

Install a drip irrigation system: this is a highly effective and water-wise way of going about things as it waters gently and over a long period. An irrigation system for your containers is an even better idea (and you can get simple kits that are easy to set up – even I can do it).

The main thing is to pay attention to watering when you are planting anything new; if you water properly when you introduce a plant, its roots will grow down towards the water table and it shouldn't need any help after that except in the severest of droughts.

Watering in the early morning or late evening is essential in the summer to reduce evaporation.

Finally, have a saucer beneath every single pot. This alone will make your life immeasurably easier.

SPRUCE
....

Tidying

In the summer garden tidying recedes into the background –
all the glory of a garden in full bloom will distract the eye from
anything less lovely and it becomes more about keeping glasses
and picnic detritus cleared away until the next lot of people
come round. My tip here is to keep a storage box or plastic
laundry basket in the shed or somewhere near the door to
collect everything up in one go. Tablecloths and cushions and
throws can live in the shed at this time of year as it's not damp.

Absent gardening

If you're going away, here is my guide to keeping things watered
and alive for your return.

Established gardens will survive perfectly well without you,
but anything in pots will need a little forward planning to get
them through your holidays. If you've persuaded someone to
be the guardian of your Eden, train them up with a degree of
nonchalance so as not to put them off. The job should be as easy
and quick as possible, so it's a good idea to group all containers
as close together as possible, and as near as possible to a source
of water. If there is no human available, then I would heartily
recommend a drip-feed irrigation kit with a timer. These are
excellent for small groups of containers, or flowerbeds that are
still establishing themselves, and are not as befuddling as you
might think to set up – especially now that everything is
explained by kind people who put videos up on YouTube.

Put houseplants in the bath

Before you go away, wet a large bath towel completely and lay it flat in the bath. Then go and find all your houseplants (obviously not your desert-hailing ones, but all the ones originating from rainforests or humid/wet environments) and put them on the towel for the duration of your holiday. All other plants simply need watering well prior to departure.

Thinning fruit

If you have a plum or other fruit tree you may notice it is chock full of fruit. If you take some of this fruit off, then what remains will be bigger and better. Definitely worth doing. Here are the rules.

We lucky custodians of fruit trees often miss out on their bounty. Either the fruits are too small, or we have left them too long, or the harvest is so vast as to be overwhelming. Even if you're an ace harvester, thinning can make the process a lot easier, and the tree will be less likely to suffer the effects of over-bearing, which can lead to biennial bearing (where the tree only fruits every other year), or the breaking of branches due to the weight of the fruit.

Start by removing any and all fruit that doesn't look perfect, and then wait for the tree to finish its own thinning procedure (the June drop), after which you can get in there with the following in mind. For cooking apples, you're looking at leaving one fruit every 15–20cm (6–8in), a little less for eaters. Pears can be thinned down to two fruits per cluster. Pluck plums with abandon, leaving just one or two every 15cm (6in). It may all seem like a bit of a production, but ultimately it's a huge amount more fun than picking up rotten fruit in the freezing cold, especially when you could have eaten it in a pie.

CHOP

Harvesting veg

Are you picking away? There's little point in bothering to sow and raise seeds, prevent them from being eaten by slugs or sat-upon by children or pecked-at by birds only to miss the very fruits of your labours. Daily five-minute forays are key here. Go out with your scissors, inspect, pluck or snip but don't leave them languishing.

Chopping perennials for a second flush

Certain herbaceous perennials, like hardy geraniums, will respond well to a bit of a chopping at this time of year if you haven't already gone at them (see Chelsea chop, page 73). You'll get fresh green new foliage (always welcome during the parched months of summer) and probably a new flush of flowers. Always water after chopping, and if you're at all worried then just chop half of the plant and see what happens. You may be pleasantly surprised.

NURTURE

Edging plants

Every year I make a special promise to myself that I'm going to move a few things backwards, and edge all the borders with something suitably low-growing and rampant – something that will withstand my mower, so I don't have to spend time corseting up the overflowing perennials at the front of my borders before each mow. So, for brilliant, low-growing, bounce-back prettiness:

Erigeron karvinskianus, the prettiest of all daisies, which can even become like a weed (although only if you dislike clouds of loveliness setting up shop in every nook and cranny).

Alchemilla mollis is another easy perennial with the loveliest growth habit, throwing up those glorious droplet-holding leaves in beautiful hummocky mounds before topping everything off with acid-green flowers.

Alpine strawberry is easy to grow from seed (see pages 48–49) and will spread obligingly, as well as being evergreen and edible to boot.

Geraniums; *G. sanguineum* forms the sweetest mounds and is a fine contender for standing up to a bad mowing technique.

FUSS

All the deadheading needs to
happen now (see pages 86–87),
but please do it with a hat on
... and a glass of wine ...
and your friends.

Tie-in

Keep those bits of string in your pocket! This is the prime time
for tying-in lost shoots and gently coaxing your climbing plants
to go where you want them to go. Without help from you
they'll just head directly upwards and you may not want that.
Five minutes of tying-in every day will make a vast difference to
your garden. Think roses, wisteria, clematis, vines, cucumbers,
winter squash and courgettes.

A summer holiday for your houseplants

Pretty much all of your houseplants will benefit greatly if you
can give them a summer holiday outside. Improved light levels,
air circulation and rainwater are all beneficial to them. You do,
however, need to make sure that those hailing from rainforest

climes are given adequate shade. Dappled is ideal (under a tree) but a porch or other partially shady area will also do, so as not to scorch the leaves. Shelter from draughts is also important, so keep them by a wall, away from drying or chilly winds. Succulents and cacti can adorn an outdoor table and soak up as much sun as they can get. Keep up with the watering and feeding; outside conditions mean that you may need to water more or less frequently. The nice thing, though, is that you can drench plants, in proper rainforest fashion when they're outside (and you may be watering your houseplants in the bath already) without moving them.

Project: How to help wildlife in hot weather

Here are a few suggestions that will take less than five minutes or no time at all.

Put some bricks or a ramp into your pond or pool, to help frogs get in and out.

Put small dishes of water out in the garden. Fill them with stones so that insects can land on them and drink

Don't tidy! Plant debris covers damp earth underneath. Keep your meddling hands, for once, to yourself.

Check your compost heap and moisten it if it's dry.

Group your containers together, creating a damp microclimate. Frogs love to hide somewhere cool and damp and out of sight.

Clearing your pond algae

It's the time of year when algae will be on its A game – warm weather and anything but the perfect chemical balance means that most of us either have ponds that look like green soup or with its surface covered in the stuff. No short-term solution is foolproof, but manually removing any blanket weed using a pole is a good start. A submerged bag of barley straw will help to prevent growth, and if you don't mind your water being black, then a pond dye is a real option as it prevents photosynthesis.

In essence though, an algae-free pond is all about achieving a delicate balance. In the long term, the solution is to ensure that any water added to your pond or pool is rainwater (I know, not always possible), that clippings, fallen leaves, mowings and compost are kept out of it, and prevented from adding nutrients, and that it has a modicum of shade. Achieving the right amount of oxygen, nutrient levels and light is a continual project; your oasis of water will always be a work in progress. Most of all, you can remove surface pond algae in five-minute bursts, as and when you see it. This is by far the most effective method of keeping it under control.

August

'In summer, the song sings itself.'
William Carlos Williams

It's August, and if your garden isn't feeling a bit fallow and brown and, well, spent, then stop reading here and go for a well-earned snooze. Seriously, this is not a busy time in the garden ... unless of course you want it to be.

SPRUCE

Tidying the late summer mess can feel insurmountable without a clear list of priorities, so here are a few tasks that fall into the low-effort/big impact category and are a good place to start.

- **Get rid of anything brown** that doesn't look gorgeous first, cutting back your spent perennials, observing down the stem and to the base, for a place to cut that will afford you a possible new flush of flowers.
- **The brown, frazzled, older leaves** of your edging and filling plants, such as *Alchemilla mollis*, can also be removed individually; a bit of time doing this detailed work will instantly lift the garden.

Bindweed removal

Perhaps you thought it was a pretty vine doing rather well in your garden, and then you started noticing it was choking every other plant in the border. Yes, it's bindweed and here's how to remove it without driving yourself mad or using weed-killer.

You will need a widger tool (this looks like a long trowel and is the perfect thing for chasing the brittle roots through the soil), a kneeler and lots of patience. A good audiobook is essential, and can turn this kind of work into a total pleasure, particularly when you end up with a large pile of white bindweed roots at the end of a session.

Depending on the time of year, your bindweed may be scrambling over and strangling your plants. Unwind it (you'll need to cut and untwine at the same time) until you get to the ground. Don't be discouraged by the number of stems. Concentrate on doing one at a time. Gently and slowly begin to

chase the roots through the soil, holding the stem
with one hand and using the widger to loosen the
soil with the other. Be super, super gentle. You don't
want the root to break, as it will create another plant
– make it a game to get as far down the root as
possible without breaking it. Sometimes you'll get to
the end of it and this is a cause for much celebration!
Sometimes you won't, and that's okay … you've
removed lots of the plant, and it'll take energy and
time for it to start again.

If the bindweed has got itself tangled within the roots
of a beloved plant, then it's sometimes a good move
to dig that plant up, wash the roots off and remove
the bindweed that way. This should be a last resort
though, and you can mostly keep things manageable
just by removing as much as possible on a regular
basis. Eventually, if you keep going, you will weaken
the plant sufficiently so that it just doesn't bother
coming back any more. That means staying open to
weeding it out whenever you see a shoot. Once you've
got that in your head, then it's easy. I swear.

If you have warm, dry weather, this is the perfect opportunity to paint garden furniture for instant mood-changing effect. Do not shy away from bright or deep colours; they tend to work much better than sludgy, receding tones, (unless of course you're trying to hide an eyesore).

Less finicky, but equally rewarding, a simple sweep of paved areas can lift any garden (not to mention its owner's spirits) in five minutes, and it's this general tidying up – putting those pots away, reeling in the hosepipe, actually planting out languishing impulse garden-centre purchases – that will bring the garden back to life again, ship-shape and ready for autumn.

CHOP

Mowing

Unless there is much rain, you may need to ease up on the mowing altogether in order to prevent your lawn from going an unsightly shade of brown. If this has happened please don't fret; the grass will recover as soon as the rains return – it's not dead. Keep watering only the things that need it. Your lawn will be fine as it is.

Do a regular sweep for small, pesky weeds that will steal light and nutrients from your darlings while you dawdle. It needn't be a chore; just use a little hand hoe on a dry day, leaving the cut weedlings to desiccate on the surface of the soil, or simply try tugging – weeds like chickweed will come out easily with a quick pull.

Apples

If you want to store apples, then you'll need to pick them slightly under-ripe. Store them in a cool place, with good air circulation and make sure they aren't touching one another. As a general rule, keep on top of tidying away windfalls and picking ripe apples (which should come away from the tree easily with a gentle twist).

Conifer clip

If you have conifers and want to clip them, then don't delay. If you leave it too late then the new young shoots will hit frost then they'll go brown and yucky. Always, always check for wildlife before you cut anything in the garden.

Flowers to pick

This is the time of year when blues and greens give way to yellows and oranges. There is so much to gather for the vase. Here are some of my favourites.

- *Rudbeckia*
- *Echinacea*
- *Aster*
- *Verbena bonariensis*
- *Dahlia*

All of the above need 'conditioning', to give them a long vase life. Have a vase ready with water in it, and a pot of simmering water. Cut them as early in the morning as possible, with a bucket of water right there as you cut, so that you can plunge the stems into it immediately. Cut the stems to the right length, again endeavouring to keep them as submerged as possible at all times. Then put the cut ends into the very hot water for 30 seconds to seal them, and then straight into your vase.

Chop your lavender

Towards the end of this month, or sometime next month (if you are in a mild area), chop your English lavender again, this time by two-thirds, giving it time to harden up for the winter. For less hardy lavenders (*Lavandula × intermedia*, *L. stoechas*) don't even think of pruning brutally like this – just remove flowers after they've gone over and shape them gently.

NURTURE

If you have any bare areas in the garden, consider sowing a green manure – it will reduce the impact of weeds and improve the structure of the soil, making it beautifully workable when you come to tackle it next year. The choice is huge – *Phacelia*, sweet clover, field beans, mustard, vetches, to name but a few.

It's okay to tire of things

Around about this time of year, my sweet peas, and some other plants, start to grate on my nerves ... they're past their best and I'm frankly bored of them. I've often been in the position where I've felt it incumbent on me to squeeze every last morsel of produce or flower from an annual plant. But if it's no longer giving you pleasure, that's really a false economy. Better by far to compost the thing and get on with one's life.

FUSS
....

Keep an eye on large-flowered beauties like dahlias and lilies, and stake them to prevent the stem buckling under the weight of those blooms. Plunging a bamboo cane next to the plant (avoiding its roots) is perfectly adequate and will keep the border looking gorgeous for longer. The cane will recede as long as its top doesn't peek above the flowers. Alternatively, pick the flowers as they appear and put them in a vase. Deadheading dahlias should be done by following the spent flower down to the base of its stem and snipping there. This will produce more flowers, both on the plant, and in your home. Win-win.

Start a compost heap

A word: compost is not for everyone. Good compost takes commitment, and you may justifiably feel that outsourcing this particular one to the council is the best option for you, but the joy making your own is unending. Equally unending are the rules governing the making of it, most of which you can ignore in favour of following your intuition, once you know that you need to create enough heat inside the heap to break down all the stuff into crumbly goodness. To get heat, you need microbial activity, so in the end, it's all about creating the best feast for these invisible guests. Once things heat up, then other microorganisms, along with worms, come in and eat the decomposing matter, and excrete the finished product.

Choose a container that works for you and your garden:
start with a layer of twiggy prunings to keep air circulation
up, and begin. Balancing your nitrogen-rich greens (soft plant
material and raw veg scraps) and carbon-rich browns (bits of
cardboard, coffee-grounds and snipped-up woody material) is
key. Cut things up small (smaller than you think you need to),
and add them to your heap in thin layers, so that there's never
too much of one thing. No cooked food, raw meat or fish
(this will attract rats and foxes), and absolutely no perennial
weeds, ever.

After this, just follow your gut. If things seem too dry, add
water; if they're too wet, add in dry stuff. With a little patience,
and a healthy dose of obsessiveness, black gold will be yours.
See pages 20–21 for advice on turning your compost.

Keep feeding
Container plants and hanging baskets are nowhere near
finished doing their stuff so keep feeding, deadheading and
watering them for maximum impact until they are suddenly
finished off by the first frosts.

Tying-in
You'll have been tying stuff in now for a while, but it's worth
knowing how to do it 'properly'. First, use a good long length of
string (at least 40cm/16in). You don't want the plant tied too
tightly to the stake, and you also want the option to add new
growth into the ring of string as it appears. First tie the string
tightly to the stake with a knot. Then tie the string around the
plant, loosely. This will keep the plant upright without
strangling or damaging it.

Project: Install a water butt

It'll be autumn soon, and it'll start to rain. If you haven't already got a water butt, then high summer is the very best time to put one in, so you don't miss all that lovely rain that's about to fall.

A water butt is an absolute boon if you have anywhere with containers that need watering regularly in the summer. It will save you money over time, and it has the added benefit of making you feel deeply virtuous every time you use it. There are many options, from faux lead and terracotta, to great hulking plastic green barrels, all of which come with fitting instructions and promise to be 'easy to install', which is probably true, if your guttering and down-pipe leads to the area in which you are prepared to have sight of a big (or small) barrel. This is not always the case, and you may have to reroute the guttering and budget accordingly.

My water butt is a vast, ugly plastic green thing, but the pleasure I get from having a constant stream of clear, gushing rainwater at my disposal far outweighs the pain of looking at it.

September

It may feel like summer still, but that's all going to change so fast. As soon as the first of the leaves start to colour there will be a palpable shift in energy; not so much a winding down, as a change in direction. Put it this way: if you'd been partying all summer you'd need a period of quiet, of refuelling, of inward (or underground) growth. That's just what the plants are beginning to do, shifting their energies from blooms to root systems, and that's why this month can be the busiest in the gardening calendar. September really is the new January.

SPRUCE

Husbandry

My favourite five-minute fling – just pick a corner and go at it. In September that probably means sweeping – perhaps the rains haven't started yet, and things are rather dry and dusty, or perhaps the leaves have started to fall, and you want a clear terrace for your last-minute sunbathing. Whatever your reasons, there's never not a good time to tidy. Some of my favourite September husbandry forays include using a leaf-blower to get dirt out of nooks and crannies that can't be reached using a brush, and removing or reducing large clods of earth in the flowerbed to make it ready for seed sowing.

Five-minute weeding is always needed, whether your garden is huge or on a window-sill. As always, take a small area (see the hula-hoop method on page 172) and clear it carefully and diligently for five minutes, marvelling at what you have achieved in so little time.

Proper weeding

If you're digging up plants (see below) then you may as well use the opportunity and take five minutes to inspect the root ball for couch grass or bindweed or creeping buttercup and remove them once and for all before you replant. Satisfaction level: off the chart.

Watering

If you plant things, do bear in mind that the ground will be very dry – it's the end of summer, and it will take time for ample rain to reach deep down into the soil. So, make sure that you water anything you plant really well. This means that a watering can's worth is absolutely not enough. Better, if you can, to use a hose, let the water come out in a trickle and leave it there for four or five hours, so that the water can seep down deep into the soil, encouraging the roots to follow suit. If you just water the top layer of earth, those roots will naturally spread outwards rather than downwards, and you will be setting the poor thing up for failure next summer, when it will wilt and die as soon as the top layer of earth dries up. You have been warned!

Leaves

Fallen leaves need constant clearing,
which makes dealing with them
the perfect five-minute thing,
because if you do a little bit
every day it never becomes an
issue. So, get your rake and get
a few off the lawn, or find the
broom and sweep a few off the
terrace, or don a rubber glove and pick
a few off the pond. If you have lots of leaves to contend
with, then a leaf-blower is a sound idea. Do bear in mind
though, that balance is everything, and quite apart from the
noise they make, leaf-blowers can upset the cycles of insects

Leaf mould

So that you have somewhere to put those leaves, get
yourself a hessian sack, or just a large black plastic bag with
a few holes punched in the sides, and put it somewhere
accessible, ready to receive each day's offerings. Every time
you pick up a handful, pop them in the bag, and when it's
full, tie it up and leave it out of sight for a couple of years
(yes, you read that right) to form glorious, crumbly leaf
mould that makes the perfect addition to any compost mix,
or a really wonderful top dressing for your containers.

and other living things that rely on undisturbed nooks and crannies in which to hide and do their thing. Be judicious when using your blower, and zone your outside space in your head, so that there are some parts of it that never see a leaf-blower and small creatures can get on with things in peace and quiet.

CHOP

Mowing

If summer has been a scorcher then you may not have needed (or wanted) to mow at all, but with more rain comes more growth, so go cautiously and set the mower to a reasonable height. If you've cleverly left some of your lawn to grow long over the summer, keeping the birds and insects happy, and your mowing time to a minimum, it's time to think about chopping back whatever 'meadow' you have now. If you're being puritan about it, you'll need a scythe, but I value my feet, which are rather good for walking with, so I end up going at it, five minutes at a time, with a pair of lawn edging scissors, removing the excess before going over it with the mower. It's a bit like cutting off a beard I imagine, in that you have to get most of it off before you can use a razor. The result will look thoroughly hideous. I mean it. You may even cry a few real tears, but the great thing about all those bare patches is that you can make holes in the lawn with your bulb auger and plant crocuses, or fritillaries, or whatever. It's all going to be okay. PROMISE.

Pruning

Five-minute clippery should be on your mind if you have evergreen hedges or topiary, as this is a great time to give them a shape before the winter. Obviously, as it may not be possible to do everything in one go, it's absolutely fine to stagger this kind of work and keep at it throughout October and even into November if you need to. This is also the time for judicious pruning of climbing roses. Don't read any books on it – you'll just confuse yourself and waste time. Simply look at the thing and cut off the bits that don't work for you, creating a pleasing framework, and tying the remaining stems onto their support in a horizontal fashion. Done. Keep any large, thorny prunings for laying atop your flowerbeds; they do a very good job of stopping larger animals walking all over newly-sown areas.

NURTURE

Eke out summer

Pot up some mint, not only for infusions, cocktails and cooking, but because the scent encapsulates summer. All you need do is dig up a small clump and literally plonk it in a pot (or pots) of ordinary multi-purpose compost. Parsley is another candidate for this treatment.

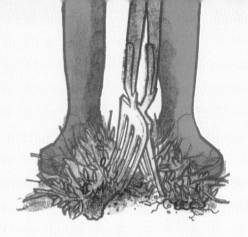

Dividing

The soil is so very warm, but top growth is slowing down – what better time than this to plant, move, or generally mess about with things? Your perennials should be the first target; perhaps you have a vast patch of hardy geraniums that could be split into two, four or six and dotted about the garden? Cut the top growth off completely, dig the plant up and get most of the soil off the roots. Now get two forks and push them into the centre of the plant right next to each other, back to back, and tease the root ball apart by pushing the two handles together. It may take a few attempts, but eventually you'll have two bits of plant, which you can then replant, or divide again.

Hippeastrum (amaryllis) downtime

It's time for your *Hippeastrum* bulbs to hibernate for a while. Move them into a cool room, stop feeding and reduce watering to a trickle (for the annual care timetable see page 143).

Plant shopping

This is a great time to go out in search of the perennials you have been yearning for, as the garden centres will struggle to sell those that are not in bloom, and therefore be discounting them.

Bulb planting

Always the headline in any September to-do list in the press, because they get to attach pictures of all the pretty tulips and daffs you'll get come the spring, but rest assured that you need not panic about getting them in – there is always October and November, and yes, there is December and January too, if you really are very behind. Tulips do better if you wait until it's cold to plant them (just go outside and if you shiver, then it's time). Having said all that, for all but your tulips, the warm, September soil will undoubtedly give bulbs a good start, so it's as well to spend five minutes getting a few in when you can. I like to use a bulb auger, which is basically a massive corkscrew that I attach to my drill. It makes lovely clean holes with minimal disruption and means I can pop bulbs into tiny spaces between plants that are still blooming.

Bulbs in containers

This is truly the most effective way of displaying bulbs; you get to put them exactly where you want them, and you don't have to worry about other plants' roots. It's as easy as tossing a load of bulbs into a container, covering them with a bit of earth, watering and waiting; the bulbs will come up, and your world will be happy. But there are a few tricks to make the bulbs perform to their maximum potential.

First, your bulb receptacle should be as large as possible. Compost should be multi-purpose, and a handful of grit beneath each bulb means they are less likely to rot off if the pot gets over-wet. Plant bulbs at roughly twice their depth (if you are layering you may need to go deeper). If you are bothering to go to all this effort, then the issue of protection from squirrels, mice, birds and the rest will need addressing. Find some form of cloche (bamboo cloches are light-weight, durable, not too expensive and good-looking, and you can cram them tightly over your containers).

I like mixing early and late tulips (for example, April-flowering 'Princess Irene', followed by May beauty 'Spring Green'), and layering them up is a good idea – put the largest bulbs in first, and try to stagger them, so that one bulb doesn't sit directly on top of another. Lastly, plant bulbs with their pointy bits facing the sky; it's just kind.

Lawn bulbs

If you have an area of longer grass in your lawn (see page 57), then it would be foolish not to lace it with bulbs for spring beauty, and whilst a lawn covered in fritillaries is the stuff of dreams, there is a balance to be struck when it comes to a lawn which must be roll-or-run-about-on-able, so stick to early-flowering bulbs, giving them a good six weeks to die back naturally and then you'll be able to mow, if you wish, with abandon.

Crocus is the obvious one, and perhaps most beautiful in a single colour; *C. tommasinianus* is a charm and seeds easily. Snowdrops look really exquisite in grass, where they are set off perfectly against the green and aren't smothered by larger-leaved neighbours. *Galanthus* 'S. Arnott' and *G.* 'Magnet' are my favourites, and their height makes them extra-suitable for the lawn. Lastly, *Anemone blanda* is a beauteous thing in a lawn and comes in white for minimalists, and blue for everyone else.

Keep things natural by beginning in one corner of the lawn and throwing a few bulbs in the air, planting them where they land. If you're happy just to plant a few, then put them in one by one with a bulb planter, ejecting the cylindrical clod back over the top of the bulb and squishing down firmly. Otherwise, if it's profusion you're after, you'll need to remove some squares of your turf and plant with a trowel as naturally as possible, not forgetting to put a few bulbs right at the edge.

Seed sowing

Seed sowing is not just for spring. You only have to look at nature to understand that most flowers drop their seeds in the autumn, so it makes sense to follow her example, particularly if you want early flowers and stronger plants. My favourite seeds to sow right now are *Ammi majus*, *Nigella*, marigolds and, of course, sweet peas. Some seeds, (like *Ammi*) want to be sown 'in situ' (where they are to flower), and this is the reason why I fuss around in my flowerbeds creating a good environment for seed sowing. Others, like marigolds and sweet peas, can be sown in pots and then carefully planted out in the spring. And then there are those, like *Nigella*, which you can literally just fling about and they'll be happy.

Whatever you do though, do bear in mind that you'll need to nurture these babies over the winter, protecting them from slimy things and too much frost. Begin by weeding thoroughly and getting the soil texture nice and fine so as to allow the tiny developing roots good access to water and nutrients. Cornflower, *Nigella*, *Ammi majus*, *Eschscholzia*, *Cerinthe*, *Scabiosa* and *Calendula* are all dependable, obliging and need very little fussing over.

For a natural look (and who wouldn't want that?) mix all your seeds together before you sow

Sowing sweet peas

The easiest, most obliging seeds to sow – get these in now, and overwinter them. Sowing sweet peas in the spring is fine, but the plants will never be as big and strong and bountiful as those sown in the autumn.

First, soak your seeds overnight in warm water and then prepare some deep pots. These can be made from old loo rolls, stood up, soldier-like in a tray, or you can buy deep pots, or 'rootrainers' for the purpose. Depth is important, as sweet peas like a nice deep root run. Fill the containers with multi-purpose compost (remove the lumps) and tap the contents down to make sure there aren't any large air pockets. Plant your seeds, one to a container, 1cm (⅜in) or so deep and cover with a seed tray cover or propagator hood until they germinate. Remove the lid and get them outside quicksticks to harden off (see page 42), as they have a long cold winter ahead of them.

Poke a wooden kebab stick next to each seed, to tie the plants to once they're big enough. When they have a few leaves, pinch out the leading shoot to make the plants even stronger (see page 163). The set-up here should mean that your seedlings are protected from bad weather but not so much the cold. I keep mine in a cold frame, so I can shut the lid if it's hailing or raining hard, or snowing.

them. Some gardeners like to scatter the seeds directly over the surface of the soil and then carefully rake it. For small patches though, a little more control is needed, so I make very shallow trenches, about 15cm (6in) apart with my fingers (the lines won't be recognisable when the plants appear), and dispense the seeds very sparingly within each one. Cover each seed-filled trench over gently, and then just buzz off and get on with your life. As soon as seedlings appear, thin them out (awful but necessary, see pages 64–65) so that each plant has 10–15cm (4–6in) of space around it, and you will be rewarded for your efforts with rainbow glory to fill next year's awkward post-tulip/pre-perennial gap.

Plant up some winter containers

This is a controversial one, because rule number one of *The 5 Minute Garden* says you need to keep the number of pots to a minimum. Instead of new pots then, concentrate on under-planting any shrubs or climbers that you already have in large pots with your choice of all the delicious things there are to play with in the nurseries right now – I'm talking not just of cyclamen, but of *Viola*, heather and ornamental cabbages – all of which will add colour and fun to your terrace, balcony or window-box. My tip here is to stick to one plant only and put it everywhere, and if you are planting up new containers, then be kind to yourself and put bulbs underneath whatever goes on top. You'd be mad not to.

FUSS

Houseplant hibernation

If you've had your darlings outside for a summer holiday, then take five minutes to inspect them for any pests, and act accordingly (a jet of water is often the best way to deal with any critters). Soon you'll be bringing them indoors again for the colder months, but make the most of any remaining warm weather before you do so. Lower light levels will be beginning to slow growth for all houseplants now, so begin to reduce their watering and feeding from now on.

Five-minute wipe

Gently clean off any dust that has collected on the foliage of your indoor plants with a damp cloth. Dust can prevent light from getting in though the leaves and have a marked effect on growth, so make this ritual a fortnightly thing if at all possible.

Planning for tender plants

Last winter I got caught out by the sustained, severe weather (in April) and ended up on a wild goose chase for horticultural fleece to keep some vulnerable plants cosy during the cold snap. Take five minutes to order some fleece, and unearth your store of old bubble wrap, or order some hessian so that all these materials will be at your fingertips for wrapping and cossetting should the weather turn beastly. Think of it like one of those emergency food stores, with everything you'll need for the Apocalypse, and make sure you include string, box tape or ties of some sort. Put it all away on a shelf or in a cupboard, and then (and this is hugely important) make a note of where you've put it all, and stick the note on your fridge. Job done.

Project: A pot of bulbs for indoors

Plant up some containers for your home, to get you through the winter months. Tiny bulbs, like crocuses, and *Iris reticulata* lend themselves beautifully to this project, as you get to watch them grow and flower in close-up, and at nose level – no getting down on your hands and knees in the wet and cold to admire. You need:

- a wide shallow container (or 'pan') with drainage holes
  Note: you can do this using pretty ceramic bowls but there is the issue of knowing how much to water, so drainage holes are better if it's your first time.
- multi-purpose compost
- horticultural grit or gravel to top dress

Fill your pot with compost and gently push the bulbs in, close together but not touching and with their pointy heads just peeping out of the soil.

Water well, and then top dress with gravel – this will prevent evaporation, keep things clean when you bring the pot indoors, and it just looks nicer.

Put the bulbs in a cold dark place to make them think it's already winter and force them to start growing. Once those fresh green spears are 4–5cm (1½–2in) long, bring the pot indoors into the warmth and the light, and flowering will eventually commence.

Tying-in

Keep doing it, every time you are out in your garden, and if possible, gently add new growth into existing string rings.

Wash some pots

You're going to start removing some of your summer things from their containers round about now, and some of these pots will now remain unused until next year. Rather than just putting them away, it's a really good idea to brush them clean with a stiff bristle brush and give them a quick wash in hot soapy water. You just need a bucket, some rubber gloves, and some September sunshine to dry your pots once they've been dunked and scrubbed. You'd be hard pushed to find a jollier way to spend five minutes, I promise.

October

*'Bittersweet October. The mellow, messy,
leaf-kicking, perfect pause between the
opposing miseries of summer and winter.'*
Carol Bishop Hipps

The back-to-school vibe is strong within me, but I'm mostly too busy with actual back-to-schooling to spend any meaningful time getting the garden ship shape. Instead, it's usually October before any of that happens – the rain arrives and it's time to put away the cushions for a while.

SPRUCE

Rakery

Do you have a lawn? If you do, then you need to own a rake. I'm talking about a spring tine rake – with prongs that look a bit like spider's legs. The beauty of raking in autumn is that you can kill two birds with one stone; you can remove fallen leaves from your lawn and scarify it at the same time. Scarifying feels like an odd thing to do to a lawn. You pull the rake along the grass, pressing down firmly in one direction all over the lawn, turn around 90 degrees, and then do it again. You remove all the dead bits of grass and moss and leaves – all the stuff that's preventing light, air and water from accessing the roots of the

grass. You're going to make a terrible mess doing this, and your lawn is going to look horrific. Fret not, it will be worth it, and your lawn will be all the better for it. Oh, and keep some of that thatch – it makes excellent kindling for your autumn and winter fires (see page 148). Controversially, you could indeed decide that a mossy lawn is a thing of great beauty and leave it (and the obsession with a perfect sward) alone.

Aerating fun

This is the most underrated bit of fun you can have during a five-minute break, and I'm not sure why more people don't don a pair of spikey sandals over their shoes and tramp purposefully over their lawns looking very odd indeed – or is it just me? Anyway, grass roots are helped along massively when you put lots of small holes in the ground, allowing water and air to penetrate direct to them. You can, of course, hire machines, or use a garden fork, but lawn aerating sandals are quicker and easier – I can do my whole lawn in a couple of five-minute bursts and scroll Instagram at the same time; let them stare, I say.

Tentative tidying

A gentle plea here, for a little 'mess' (if you can call it that).
The seedheads of your perennials should stay where they are
for as long as possible. They give you something to look at, the
birds something to eat, and insects somewhere to hide. It's
understandable and fine to remove things if they look hideous,
but do think twice before you make everything super-orderly. If
you are a person who really must have everything immaculate,
consider leaving just one corner of your space untouched – it
could just be a pile of leaves – for all these beneficial creatures.

Leaf life

Pick up those leaves – daily – and plonk them inside a
pre-prepared bag for making into leaf mould (see page 123).

Five-minute Halloween décor

It's for the kids really, but the whole Halloween thing –
pumpkins and chrysanthemums at the door – does tend to
grow on us, and my feeling is that generally the less tasteful the
better. Having said that, though, this is not something I find
myself happy to splash the cash on, because, well, winter is
coming, and with it, Christmas. The best way by far is to amass
a small collection of plants from your garden or balcony or
terrace (and yes, digging stuff up is fine here, particularly if
said thing needs dividing, or is outgrowing its space). Put
everything in decorative pots (don't bother actually planting
unless you're creating a long-term display) and simply add
pumpkins. The gaudy orange ones are marvellous for carving,
but there are knobbly, multi-coloured pumpkins and gourds
aplenty, which taste rather better in the bowl once they've
made the transition from stoop to soup.

Houseplant TLC

For most houseplants you'll want to reduce watering at this time of year. Succulents and cacti have all that moisture captured in their leaves, and growth is slowing; if you water too much, the plant will be unhappy, so be very cautious. The rest need a gradual reduction in water. It's a balancing act to be honest, as the central heating is more often than not going up at this time, drying the air out. As a general rule, wait until the top of the compost is completely dry before you water, and never let these plants' roots sit in water. Plants that love humidity (like maidenhair ferns or orchids) can sit on a tray of pebbles filled with water to keep the moisture levels in the air up. Winter-flowering houseplants however, such as Chinese jasmine, should be watered frequently as they are just about to enter into active growth at this time.

NURTURE

Bulb lasagne

This is a rather strange way of describing a pot-full of layered bulbs (but it's caught on, so who am I to argue?) It's a perfect way to plant bulbs, especially if you are short on space, and you need only use one pot rather than three or four. The trick is to choose bulbs that flower at different times, creating a long season of colour and excitement (see page 128).

Lawn bulbs

While you're messing with the lawn, and if you didn't manage to get any bulbs in last month, then there's still lots of time to make it happen (see page 129).

Succulent centrepieces

If you're anything like me, you will
have fallen prey to a myriad of little
pots in the garden centre, under the
impression that you have room for
'just one more'. The problem is, you
don't, and this is particularly true if
you are time-limited, so do yourself a
favour and corral your treasures together
into one larger container. It needs to be wide
and shallow, and you need a compost mix of half
multi-purpose compost and half perlite or grit. Fill the pot
half full and arrange everything together, filling in the gaps
with more compost, and top with horticultural gravel or grit,
to keep moisture away from the base of the plants. Don't water
your new arrangement immediately, but wait until you see that
one of the inhabitants needs a drink, at which point water
cautiously. This five-minute fling will bring new life to
your collection.

Paperwhites

Fresh flowers and foliage are a must for me, not just over
Christmas and New Year, but more importantly BEYOND,
when all the festivities are over, and we just have to get through
the darkness and freezing temperatures until the arrival of
spring. Timing is always a bit of a gamble with indoor bulbs,
but I tend to do three or four five-minute plantings in October
and November to cover myself. My first love is paperwhite
narcissi. The scent is sublime, and they are easy as anything to
get going. Use high-sided glass vases for a simple life, as you
won't need to support the stems, and also large gravel or

marbles rather than bulb fibre. Fill a vase with about 10cm (4in) of stones and place one, three, five or seven bulbs on top, scattering a bit more gravel over the top to keep them in place. Now water to just below the base of the bulbs (easy to see through the glass vase) and keep them in a cool dark place to start growing. Once you see action – good 5cm (2in) tall spears – then bring them indoors to flower.

Hippeastrum (amaryllis)

These are now a non-negotiable part of my winter, and, because the bulbs are expensive, I've turned the whole performance into a collection, adding one or two bulbs each year and following a simple care timetable to get them back and blooming every winter (see opposite). If this is your first time, you need to find a pot whose circumference just exceeds that of the bulb. Go for a mini long-tom pot (see pages 172–173), as this will give the roots enough to cling on to. If you're planting three or five in one pot, you're going to need something really big.

Soak the bulb in warmish water for an hour or so and plant it in a half-and-half mixture of multi-purpose and John Innes No. 2 compost with the top third above the surface, filling in around the edge so that the bulb is nice and snug. Water it well and put it indoors, somewhere cool but light. Put in pots like this, and grown on a little, these make excellent Christmas presents. The plants are magnificent indoors with their huge strappy leaves, and if I had vast amounts of space (and light) I would have all of them displayed together, but in reality I often chop the flowers when they are in bud and use them in small, low vases to decorate the kitchen or bedside table. I can then put the plant in another room and follow the timetable opposite.

Annual *Hippeastrum* care timetable

* After flowering: cut the flower spikes at the base
  and continue with watering.
* Dose with a liquid fertiliser (seaweed is fine) once a
  week. This is important for bulb replenishment, so
  that it can flower again next year.
* Once the weather is kind – June sort of kind – put the
  pots outside for a summer holiday. Be very careful to
  protect them from slugs and snails who will strip the
  leaves! Keep up watering and feeding during this time.
* At the end of September, reduce watering and stop
  feeding and move the plants into an unheated room
  by a window. This is their dormant period and it should
  last two months.
* In December, chop off the leaves close to the bulb (just
  as you see in the shops), scrape off the top 3cm (1¼in)
  of compost and replace with new, bring them into
  a warmer, brighter room and start the whole
  process again (see above).

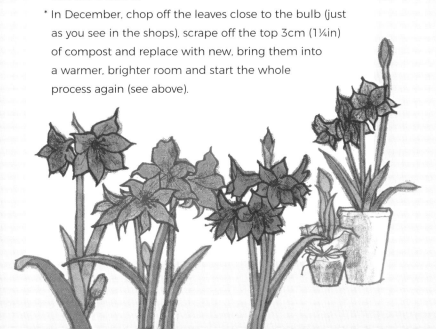

FUSS

Dahlia chop

Ugh! Can you bear it? Can you chop all this glory down?
If you can (and have a total dahlia-fest indoors with as many
vases as you can find), then you'll be doing your plants a bit of
a favour by diverting energy away from flowers and potential
seed-making and back down into the tubers. Chop just the top
third of the plant off; you need the leaves to photosynthesise
and feed the tubers.

Call the contractors

If you've been meaning to sort out some hard landscaping, or
install lighting for the winter, then now is a great time to get
on the phone and book a contractor to come and give a quote.
Work for landscapers and garden designers generally eases
off at this time of year, meaning that as well as getting their
undivided attention (let's face it, once we've decided to spend
money on something we want it done yesterday), you may also
be able to negotiate slightly on the price, bearing in mind,
of course, that everyone needs to make a profit.

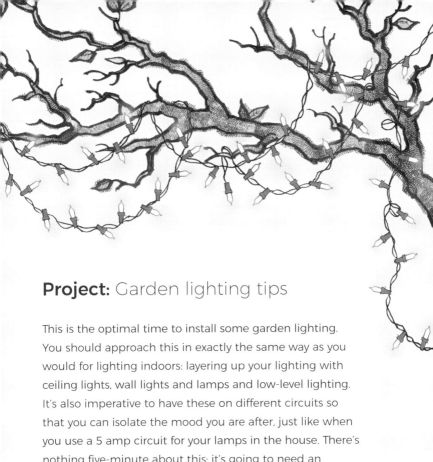

Project: Garden lighting tips

This is the optimal time to install some garden lighting.
You should approach this in exactly the same way as you
would for lighting indoors: layering up your lighting with
ceiling lights, wall lights and lamps and low-level lighting.
It's also imperative to have these on different circuits so
that you can isolate the mood you are after, just like when
you use a 5 amp circuit for your lamps in the house. There's
nothing five-minute about this; it's going to need an
electrician and some cash, but don't discount the dazzling
array of outdoor products available as Christmas lighting.
Fairy lights are a lovely way of illuminating your garden on
a budget as long as you have an outdoor socket, and even
without one, solar or battery-powered products, from fake
flickering candles to hedge netting are well worth it, if only
as a way of establishing whether putting in something
more permanent would be important to your life.

November

*'Some of the days of November carry the
whole of the memory of summer, as a fire
opal carries the colour of moonrise.'*
Gladys Taber

The beauty of November can be beyond measure, if only you will stop and stare a little; seedheads mostly, but also the joy that a little husbandry brings. Oh, and then of course there is fire.

SPRUCE

Fire and stuff

It's time to ask again 'What is your garden for?' Mine is definitely for having fun in, and I love to use bonfire night as an excuse to enjoy the garden. All I'm really talking about is a fire bowl and some hot soup; fireworks are totally unnecessary, but sparklers are essential. If you've never built a fire before, it is one of those things that makes you feel strangely independent and accomplished. A fire is also obviously useful for winter gardening and getting rid of perennial weeds that you don't want in your compost, and stuff that's too big to compost. If you love gardening, it's a good idea to make friends with fire, for all the reasons above, but mainly for the warmth of it over the winter months.

Build a great fire in a fire bowl

This method is spot on if you have children who like to 'help' – they can assemble all the wood before anything is lit. This fire needs next to nothing in terms of management once it's built and will burn for 1–2 hours.

You need wood of different sizes ranging from large pieces – 1–20cm (⅜–8in) diameter – all the way down to kindling. The best kindling is dried thatch from a lawn (see page 172) but any bone-dry vegetation will do, as long as the leaves are small enough that you can create a bundle of it about the size of a small watermelon.

Put the largest logs in a line at the bottom of the bowl, and add another layer of smaller ones in another row, at 90 degrees. Continue with this, adding each layer until you have tiny sticks and then your ball of kindling. Put a few more tiny sticks in a tepee over the top of your kindling and then light it. *Voilà!* Your fire will burn down, without you having to add bits to it as it burns.

Leaf mould

Have you set up your leaf-mould stations yet? If not, don't worry; but know that your life will be massively improved by a bag or three of rotting leaves hidden away for a couple of years. Sweeping them up and putting them in bags is easy, but somehow setting up leaf-mould stations, so that the whole thing becomes easy and un-chore-like, seems to require (for me) rather more oomph. Do it though (see page 123).

Washing paths and terraces

The frenzy of weeding having died down somewhat, you can focus your energies onto other areas, and although I am loath to mention the words 'health and safety', it's nevertheless really lovely if people can use your outside space, or walk up your steps without ending up in hospital. Green algae and other slippery stuff is easy to remove with a jet washer or scrubbing brush and some really hot soapy water. You will feel properly smug too.

Weeding paths and terraces

See above, but the cracks and crevices in paths, terraces and steps are often home to weeds that use this time of year, when most of us are not focussing on the outside, literally to put down roots. Some of them are fine – you want them there – Mexican daisy (*Erigeron karvinskianus*), lady's mantle (*Alchemilla mollis*) and houseleeks (*Sempervivum*) are examples of welcome crack guests. The others though, are squatters and now is a great time to evict them. Use a brush and a gloved hand for easy-to-remove weeds, and an old knife or screwdriver for more stubborn ones.

Winter lingering

A place to sit, or at least to perch, close to your fire bowl, and with or without a waterproof cushion or three is going to make a whole world of difference to your experience of winter. It will give you a place to escape into freshness and away from the fug of hibernation. And if you plant scented winter shrubs nearby, then so much the better (see page 14).

CHOP

Keep on chopping

As I mentioned before, there's a fine line in gardening with perennials between statuesquely chic and brown and revolting. Only you know where that line is, and it's your garden so don't let your inner bully tell you that you must chop things when you think they look lovely. You can revisit the situation every week and pick and choose what goes and what stays (see Tuesday chop, page 169). Let your instinct guide you; sedum (now called *Hylotelephium*) may have been lying prostrate for a while, with lots of new, exciting buds all coming forth from the centre ... it's a wonderful prospect and you might want to get rid of those falling-over, outer stems, especially if they're crowding neighbouring plants. If, however, you were clever enough to provide support for your plants, and prevented them from falling over, the seedheads will last much longer.

Summer bulb chop

Certainly though, get rid of the gone-over flowers of any summer bulbs you're still tending. Their leaves need to go completely brown and crispy before you lift them to store for next year, and leaving the seedhead there will deplete the bulb's energies. If you have bulbs in containers, lift them out once the leaves are brown (which could be as late as January) and put in something else (spring bulbs topped with cyclamen or hellebores are always a treat).

Container audit

Any containers that are 'gone over' (and I use the term loosely to conjure up an image of anything that is no longer doing its all-singing, all dancing, glorious thing) can now be dealt with. You might have tomatoes that have finally been got by a frost, or pots full of summer bedding that are still looking okay but are basically past their best. Take the plunge and compost these things, replacing them with winter perennials or bedding and as always, don't forget to put bulbs beneath.

NURTURE

Overwintering

Summer bulbs and tubers (dahlias, cannas, and so on) are not hardy. This means that to keep them, and be 100 per cent sure that they'll survive the winter, you'll need to lift them out of the ground, brush off the earth and store them in a cool, dry place over the cold months. It's a bit of a faff, but obviously worth it if you plan to have these plants form the backbone of your garden, and you live somewhere cold. If it's just a few summer bulbs, then it's probably a false economy to enter into the circus of storing them as they are relatively cheap to buy. Dahlias, though, are a different matter. Cut the stems to 10cm (4in) or so above the ground, and dig up the tuber, brushing off

Project: Grow some garlic

Success is crucial in gardening, where one has so little control over the elements and minibeasts that can scupper the best laid plans, and this is why I love growing garlic; it seems to work, growing and doing its thing without any coddling or worrying. You can even grow it in a container if you like (use a 50/50 mix of multi-purpose compost and John Innes No. 2 with a few handfuls of grit). You need:

· some garlic bulbs
· an area that gets a good amount of sunshine, with well-drained soil

Break some good fat cloves off from the bulbs, making sure to retain the flat bit at the bottom of each one.

Push them, flat side down, into the soil about 5cm (2in) deep and 10cm (4in) apart.

Cover them up and water if necessary, then wait.

You'll see action in early spring, with tall flowers following. I start digging up bulbs when the leaves begin to go brown.

Keep some for immediate use and hang the rest up somewhere cool so that the sap can travel down the stem and swell the bulbs over time.

excess soil. Store them for a week or so, upside down, and then do a general tidy-up, snipping off skinny 'rat's tail' tubers and any hairy bits, along with the darker 'mother' tuber from last year. Put them in a box of just-moist compost ('just moist' means that if you squeeze some in your hand it would momentarily hold together and then fall apart, leaving your hand clean) and keep them insulated against frost.

Sweet pea support

If you sowed sweet peas this year then it might be time to tie them gently to some kind of support, so they don't flop over. This is a delicate job and I usually use wooden kebab sticks, plunged into each sweet pea cell at the time of sowing. Tie them ever so gently so that each emergent seedling is leaning against an upright.

Tulip planting

Zero panicking please! Tulips prefer to be planted once the cold has frozen out some of the nasties in the soil that give them diseases. For this reason, you can play your tulip planting by ear. Let it be chilly for two or three days and then plunge them in (and yes, that could mean waiting until December).

Pumpkin soup

It's not gardening, but composting is, and eating your pumpkin is SO much better than composting it! Don't bother with peeling – just hack the thing up into large chunks and roast with olive oil and salt until you can remove the skin easily and purée it up. Then add coconut milk and *all* the spices.

FUSS

Order manure

If you don't do compost heaps (and even if you DO do them) ordering a load of manure is the ultimate early Christmas present for your outside space. Feeding the soil with an insulating, nourishing layer of horse poo will do more for your plants than all the other 'fertilisers' you can throw at them, and that's because it will not only feed your plants, but also improve the structure of the soil in the process. If you're lucky enough to have space for it, avoid plastic bags by ordering in one large 'dump' from a local stables or manure business. Otherwise, save the bags for the future; they are thick and sturdy, and can be used again and again.

How to mulch, the five-minute way

Now I understand fully how one might shrink from the idea of mulching an entire garden alone, but rest assured, it can be done. The key is in the preparation, and an acceptance that you're going to be doing one load a day for however long it takes. If you're using bags, simply dash out with a sharp knife, slash one open and tip it into a wheelbarrow or a couple of trugs. Use a trowel to sprinkle the stuff around the base of

Mulch lowdown

Mulching means adding a layer of something on top of the soil. The best mulches break down over time, get pulled downwards by worms, and improve both the structure and nutrient levels of the soil. Garden compost is an excellent mulch. Well-rotted horse manure is great too, and for most people, these are the most accessible types of nutrient rich, soil-improving mulches. The ultimate is to mulch throughout the year – putting a deep layer of muck around shrubs and trees, and on flowerbeds at regular intervals – but in practice, unless you are very lucky and have a never-ending supply of compost, it's usually easier to order a pile of manure and do it in one go.

The very best time to mulch is whenever you think of it. As long as the ground is neither too cold, nor too dry, there is never NOT a good time to pile goodness onto your soil (my excess lawn mowings go directly around the base of my shrubs over the summer). In reality though, there are too many delicate things poking out of the ground at most other times of the year, so autumn is often the most expedient time.

each and every plant (especially shrubs and trees) that you love. Make sure the layer is nice and thick (10cm/4in is great). If your manure is loose, you'll need to shovel it into your wheelbarrow or trugs first. Repeat each day until the job is done. Believe me, this will become one of your favourite enterprises once you begin. The visual pay-off is simply delicious and this, coupled with the fact that there is zero thinking involved, makes it a truly winning occupation.

Cacti watch

If you have succulents and cacti be aware of the change to their environment at this time of year as you up your heating. These plants still need water when they're in a centrally heated home.

Lighting

Stop agonising and order some solar-powered lights that you can either throw over, or drape artfully, across your hedge or topiary. Minimum fuss, maximum gorgeousness, and no electricians needed.

Order a hedge ...

I have a secret to share with you and it is this: bare-root hedging plants cost a fraction of their potted counterparts, and they thrive better to boot. Obviously, the trade-off here is that you won't get an instant hedge, but as a person who enjoys watching stuff grow, that's really not a downside at all. I mention it now, because this is the time of year when bare-root hedging is lifted from its field and sent to you to plant, so if you've always felt that a hedge would improve your space (and there are very few spaces that are NOT improved by the addition of a hedge) then now is the time to order one.

And plant it

Bare root hedging needs a bit of TLC before you put in into the ground. Soak the roots first, for a few hours, to soften them and let them know it's time to explore, and while you're doing that, dig a trench where you want your hedge to be, filling the bottom of it with a bit of manure and mixing with the existing earth. Place each plant in and carefully back-fill, applying pressure with your foot to firm the plant in. Water in really well. You need to continue watering daily for a week, and then every three days or so for another couple of weeks, encouraging the roots to seek depth rather than stay near the surface. If you water your new hedge and feed it over the growing season, it will grow really fast, and end up much better and stronger than the type of fully-formed one you re-mortgaged your house for.

Christmas

Gardening is so much more satisfying when your tools are great quality and your hands are warm, so send out your Christmas list immediately! If they don't know what you want then you aren't going to get it. Gloves are always a good idea, as are gorgeous tools that you might not feel justified in buying for yourself (although why ever not?).

Deadhead

Deadheading (or 'fussing') is still needed (even in November) if you want your blooms to renew themselves constantly. I'm thinking principally about autumn and winter bedding, like cyclamen, chrysanthemums and the like, which will perform beautifully with no interference from your thumb and forefinger but exponentially better if you do employ them. It's a one-handed thing, and best done in the light (although a foray outside in some warm clothing with a glass of something fizzy is also a good way to approach it), and if it's too chilly then gloves and a pair of scissors are definitely an option.

Leaves in the flowerbeds

There is definitely an argument for gentle removal of leaves in your flowerbeds, particularly if they are in danger of drowning out emergent bulbs and other plants. So, whenever you pass a leaf-covered container or bit of flowerbed, just spend five minutes removing a few leaves and plonking them in your nearest leaf-mould station. If you have a leaf-blower and it's a dry day, then so much the better. For extra Brownie points you could even blow them all onto a lawn and run the mower over them before adding them to your leaf mould.

Mowing the lawn

Do this sporadically, because every November is different, and
sometimes the lawn is still growing. Keep the mower on a really
high setting so as not to chop too much, and be as slapdash as
you see fit – let's face it, this is more of a leaf-hoovering exercise
really, but a highly satisfactory one at that.

Shed clear and declutter

Don't be scared; this is not a call to get your shed shiny clean.
This is simply a quick, five-minute tidy and declutter. You
might be surprised at how much you've accumulated that you
don't actually need: leftover bulbs (plant them somewhere),
gloves with holes in them (chuck them), cardboard packaging
and so on ... it all needs to go.

December

'How did it get so late so soon?'
Dr Seuss

A word

We might like to think we can keep going like machines, day in,
day out, maintaining the same levels of energy and enterprise,
but this is folly. The day's length, general light levels, and colder
temperatures have the natural effect of ushering us into the
warmth and security of our homes during the winter months.
We need to hibernate. All this to say that winter is when the
five-minute concept often really IS five minutes; it might be
better described as 'a breath of fresh air'. Gardening is meant
to be calming and restorative, not a punishing daily grind.
Go gently in all things.

SPRUCE

If you made a winter lingering area last month then you are
fully set up to host a few friends for Christmas drinks or New
Year japes. Or not; because sometimes keeping people and
parties to a minimum over this very busy season is what's
needed. The point is that your garden or balcony, or whatever
outside area you have, should serve you, and as such, there is
absolutely an argument for making sure there's a fire bowl and

a cushion ready for you and your hot chocolate and your fingerless gloves so that you can get away from Christmas fug, breathe in all the freshness, and watch your breath dissipate into the chilly air. (See page 148)

Leaf-clearing

Leaf-clearing is slowing down but still a regular thing. You are on the home stretch now, and hopefully you have a lovely fat bag or two of leaves already stashed away, depending on the level of leafery in your garden. Going outside, and getting away from Christmas heat and smells is a joy, and you may find that the festive season is the time when you do more than usual outside. Remember to put holes in the bags if they are plastic, and ensure that the leaves are damp. Put them in an out-of-the-way place and forget about them for a couple of years.

More mulching

How is the mulching going? If you haven't yet begun then go to page 154 and do the daily mulching dance until your outside space is fully covered with a thick duvet of goodness.

CHOP

Remember that gone-over plants that don't look like supermodels can be removed.

Fruit trees

If it's cold enough, you can begin tackling your apples and pears (see page 26).

Pinching out sweet peas

You may have noticed that your autumn-sown sweet peas are now displaying sideshoots and are shooting skywards alarmingly. If you pinch out the leading shoot (the one in the middle), then the plant's energy will divert to the other little shoots on the side, and you'll get more flowers and a stronger, stockier plant. Use your thumb and forefinger, or a pair of scissors, and take the top third off the plant, pinching it off just above a pair of leaves.

NURTURE

Staying snug in the winter

Hardy annuals (like sweet peas) can deal perfectly well with the cold, but you may want to give the little seedlings some protection from heavy rain and snowfall, which can break their stems. A cold frame is ideal for this, as it can be kept open, to allow proper air flow and keep the plants strong and stocky. If you don't have one though, you can use a clear plastic storage box (everyone seems to have one), and leave the lid off-centre, so that you're preventing damage to seedlings as well as keeping them cool. Otherwise, a sheltered area, where they can stay chilly but not get bashed, like a porch, is ideal.

Hippeastrum showtime

It's time to bring your *Hippeastrum* out of hibernation
and get it going again for more flowers (see page 143).

Christmas flowers, the five-minute way

Here is the easiest way to decorate your terrace and home
for Christmas, and indeed, the winter season: hellebores.
Hellebores come in a myriad of exquisite permutations.
Speckled and gorgeous in sexy bruised hues. They are
ubiquitous but somehow unexpected at the same time,
mostly because people pass them over in favour of more
flashy contenders. But if you fill a few pots with some
hellebores, perhaps adding some trailing *Muehlenbeckia* to soften
and add a cascading element, you will not only provide yourself
with a collection of permanent plantings for your terrace, but
loads of beautiful blooms with which to decorate your table
(float the flowers in bowls of water, or just bring the whole pot
indoors for a while).

FUSS
....

Christmas embellishments

If you want something a little extra on your wreath or garlands, or in your candle pots (see the project page 167), get a very tiny drill bit and carefully drill through some walnuts, threading wire through as you go. Then spray them gold or silver. Once you've made these, you'll use them every year, so they are well worth the effort, and you can respray them as many times as you like.

The best foliage for Christmas decorations

Buy it or chop it. Here is my favourite festive foliage.

* Ivy: there really is nothing more lovely, particularly if you can get the flowers which are emerging at this time of year.
* Fir: and by this I mean any type of fragrant conifer. It gives beautiful coverage for wreaths and garlands and, if you don't have a source, it's relatively inexpensive.
* Eucalyptus: glaucous, fragrant and understated.

Deadheading

Viola or pansies, cyclamen and all the rest, still need fussing
around with if you are to get the very best from them. If things
have been relatively warm, you may even still have pots of
Argyranthemum, pelargoniums or
other summer beauties on
the terrace, looking a
bit brown, but
nevertheless
making a play at
being glorious.
Either bring these
indoors (why not?)
for decoration, or
keep removing
unsightly bits from them
so they earn their place in
your space.

If the weather has given your plants a bit of a bashing, or if they
are looking drab or simply worn out (and don't we all know
that feeling), then remove them and quickly plunge some tulips
in the pots – no need to change the compost unless it's
completely root-filled.

The five-minute wreath

It's easy to gather the necessary for a homemade wreath if you
are so inclined. A bit of respectful foraging on a long walk will
usually yield much loveliness in the form of evergreens and
other beauties, such as winter jasmine or old man's beard
(clematis seedheads). Stick these through a rattan wreath form;

no wiring required. It really is the five-minute wreath, and I love the look of it, but of course there are manifold other options.

If you really can't be bothered to fiddle with a wreath, then just tie a load of foliage into a 'bouquet' and hang it upside down on your door.

Project: Five-minute Christmas table decorations

Another super-easy decoration and zero-waste hack that I use every year. You need:

· small terracotta pots filled with compost
· tall candles
· foliage (ivy, eucalyptus, fir, holly – anything you have around)

Water the compost in the pot.
Stick a candle into the middle of the pot, making sure the compost is tightly packed around it, and then push foliage around the candle, covering all the compost.
Add embellishments as you wish.
Keep these watered, and place them as much as possible in a cool room or outside, and they should last two weeks or more.

The five-minute method to keep your garden beautiful

This is the outline I follow, and I put it here simply as an idea to spark your gardening endeavours.

Everyday basics

Watering, weeding, sweeping, tidying – do as much as you can in five minutes.

Watering: all containerised plants in summer.

Weeding: pick a spot, start the timer, ready, set, go! Two trays or trugs: one for composting, the other for council or black bin.

Sweeping: sweep or blow out steps, paths and terraces. Compost leaves.

Resetting and tidying: cushions out, umbrellas up, lights and candles lit and vice versa at the end of the day.

Monday spruce

This little enterprise sets you up for your week. It's a general garden-tidying mission – all the baseline jobs but over the entire garden. Don't get into detail – no perfectionism here, but you will get round the whole area. Tidy away anything out of place, weed anything that's obvious when you look around, roughly sweep/blow all terraces, steps and paths and water anything that needs a drink.

Tuesday chop

This is everything that needs chopping and tying-in.
Get those secateurs and do the dead, diseased and
dying dance. Next, tackle any tree or shrub branches
that need pruning or shaping. Tie in anything that needs
training. Put everything into a bag for council composting,
or chop up fine for home composting. Mow and edge the
lawn (summer).

Wednesday nurture

This involves moving and planting. Take stock. Lift
and divide perennials that need it in autumn, move
(or remove) anything that's not working and replace
with something else. Sow seed, prick out, pot on,
plant out. Plant bulbs in autumn.

Thursday fuss

This is simple deadheading and fussing. Glass of wine,
finger and thumb. Compost or vase. Also feeding
containers in summer.

Project: The Friday Project

This is simply a day where I pick something that needs doing and go a bit deeper than my normal, slapdash gardening. I pick something from the list below (which is not exhaustive but covers most of the things that need attention in my own garden).

1. **Terrace or patio, steps and paths, window-sills, balconies**
   Wash with a strong hose stream or pressure wash and/or scrub with baking soda/vinegar to remove any slippery mould. Weed between cracks.
2. **Lawn**
   Weed out any dandelions. Deal with any bald or yellow patches.
3. **Flowerbeds**
   Get between the plants and search out hidden weeds, prune out any dead, diseased or dying matter, deadhead in summer, divide in autumn, mulch in winter.
4. **Containers**
   Re-pot in spring, feed and deadhead in summer, plant up in autumn and spring, mulch, weed, and so on.
5. **Topiary**
   Clip, feed, mulch according to season.
6. **Compost**
   Turn the heap, add green or brown waste/bulking agents, and so on.

7. **Tools and shed, greenhouse**
   Tidy away anything that's out of place, brush down
   surfaces, clean and sweep/wash floors.

8. **Pond or water features**
   Remove weeds and/or fallen leaves, add oxygenators.

9. **Indoor plants**
   Wipe leaves to remove dust, turn plants, pot on or
   propagate as necessary.

10. **Garden furniture**
    Brush down and wipe clean.

If you have a huge job that needs doing quickly, simply add
it to your basic list, and do it instead – so, for example, you
could make mulching the garden your basic enterprise for
an entire week – a trug-full a day.

Glossary

Aeration (lawns): Putting lots of small holes in the ground to allow water and nutrients to get into the grass roots. You can hire machines, or use a garden fork, but lawn aerating sandals are quicker, easier and much more fun (see page 138).

Bedding (plants): Plants grown specifically for a spring, summer or winter display, planted into garden beds or containers, and discarded at the end of the season.

Deadheading: If you remove flowers before they fade and set seed, the plant will produce more of them. The more going-over flowers you chop, the more new and beauteous flowers your plants will produce. Simple. Add a feeding regime to help the plant out and you will have a continual display.

Hardening off: Acclimatising some of your baby or tender plants to outdoor temperatures (see page 42 for method).

Hardy plants: A plant that is able to withstand seasonal drops in temperature during the winter is hardy and, depending on the plant, will be able to survive year after year despite adverse growing conditions such as frost or cold winds.

Hula-hoop method: The best, and least overwhelming way to tackle weeding is via the square metre or 'hula-hoop' method. Use a hula hoop to mark out a small area for weeding. Five minutes a day, one area. Go, go, go!

Lawn thatch: The dead bits of grass and moss (thatch) covering your lawn that prevent light, air and water from accessing the roots of the grass. Rake in April or October and remember to set some thatch aside – it makes the best kindling for fires.

Leaf-mould station: Keep your rotting leaves hidden away for a couple of years to form glorious, crumbly leaf mould. Punch a few holes in the side of a large plastic bag and place somewhere accessible. Every time you sweep or pick up a handful of leaves, pop them in the bag. When full, tie it up and leave it to do its thing.

Long tom: Quality traditional long tom pots are taller and narrower than usual plant pots and are most suitable for taller plants, such as lilies.

Micro-greens: A seed tray of fast-growing plants that you can snip regularly for use in cooking, such as radish, rocket, basil, coriander and mizuna (see page 19).

Mulch: Adding a layer of garden compost, well-rotted horse manure or other nutrient rich, soil-improving material on top of the soil (pages 154–156).

Perlite: A volcanic material that is very useful when added to compost to plants that need an extra-light growing medium, such as when growing seeds, or potting up houseplants.

Potting on: When a young plant or seedling outgrows its pot and needs a larger one.

Pricking out: Separating seedlings and transferring them so that they have more space to grow on (see pages 64–65).

Re-potting: When any plant outgrows its pot and needs a larger one.

Scarifying: Pull a spring tine rake along the grass, pressing down firmly in one direction all over the lawn, turn around 90 degrees, and then do it again to remove dead grass (thatch, see above).

Thinning: Removing fruits at various places to encourage the ones left behind to grow bigger, or removing overcrowded seedlings in order to give their neighbours enough space to reach their full potential.

Top-dressing: Removing the top 5cm (2in) of soil and replacing it with new to provide the plant with added nutrients.

Tying-in: Keeping a climbing plant growing where it's supposed to, by tying shoots to the wall or support with string (see page 118).

Index

Acknowledgements

Making a book is a team sport. To my editors, Katie Bond at National Trust and Peter Taylor at Pavilion, thank you for your enthusiasm and expertise. Being commissioned is always unbelievable and I am continually thrilled that you were as taken with this crazy idea as I was!

To the brilliant Kristy Richardson who has worked with me to make this little gem just as we envisioned, my heartfelt thanks for your excellence and your patience, and also to Claire Masset – how lucky I am to have a gardener and writer in the mix.

Huge thanks to Liane Payne whose illustrations have brought this book to life; what a treat to have ones words augmented so beautifully, and to Tokiko Morishima at Pavilion for the beautiful design of this book; I am so grateful.

This book was born on Instagram, where I began to document my daily five minute gardening forays, so I must thank all of my kind, generous Instagram friends for their support and encouragement; without you I would never have thought of putting it all down on paper.

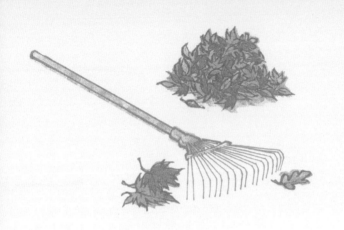